I0157657

OUT

OF

DARKNESS

THE MANIFESTATION OF THE SONS OF GOD

RUSSELL RAIA, JR.
AND GINA RAIA

Out of Darkness – The Manifestation of the sons of God

Copyright © 2017 Russell Raia, Jr. and Gina Raia

Published in the United States of America 2017 by Anathoth Publishing, The Church At Houston, Inc., Houston, Texas www.thechurchathoustonlive.org

Unless otherwise indicated, all Scripture taken from the NEW AMERICAN STANDARD BIBLE. Copyright 1960, 1962, 1963, 1968, 1971, 1972, 1973, 1975, 1977, 1995 by the Lockman Foundation. Used by permission. www.Lockman.org.

Scripture found on Page 213 is taken from the Amplified Bible, Copyright © 1954, 1958, 1962, 1964, 1965, 1987 by the Lockman Foundation. Used by permission.

Artwork found on page 157 and page 235 is taken from cliparts.co; a href="http://cliparts.co">Clip arts</a>. Used by permission.

ISBN: 978-0-692-96576-4.

PREFACE

As a means of introduction of the authors to the reader, we are persons given over to the Divine thought of our heavenly Father - that He has in each of us a dwelling place, a place of His rest. That place is Christ. He alone is the place of God's rest. We having seen the Messiah are now being built as that dwelling place of God through the sanctifying work of the Holy Spirit, to Whom we presently surrender. As we completely surrender to the lordship of the Holy Spirit, it becomes Christ alone who lives in us, thus we become as Christ unto the Father, a place of His rest.

As children of God, born again into His family, we declare to live by every word that proceeds from the mouth of the Lord. Not that we have already obtained it [that place of sonship, since sonship is evidenced by the life that can do nothing apart from the Father] or have already become perfect, but we press on so that we may lay hold of that for which also we were laid hold of, by Christ Jesus, our Lord – to be a son of God, perfect and complete, lacking in nothing.

By way of our testimony [the evidence of our life, lived], we shall declare to all men the Divine thought, and with all diligence, as one enlisted as a soldier, take what we have received to those to whom He sends us. And this is what we have received; that the Almighty God has come to dwell within man, to make for Himself sons, that He may with them share His glory. To be that dwelling, one must be made from above, made from heaven, by God's own hand. It is for this, God indwelling man, that all of creation is anxiously longing.

Therefore, we continuously look upon the cross of Christ as representing the death of everything that we were and are and look upon the risen and exalted Christ as possessing everything that we are and will be in the mind of God.

Finally, our deepest love and appreciation is extended to our brothers and sisters of the Church at Houston whose continuing labors to be pleasing to the Father have allowed us to witness the work of God in the lives of men.

To our brothers and sisters, as always, it is our prayer that *"you may [continue to] be filled with the knowledge of His will in all spiritual wisdom and understanding, so that you will [continue to] walk in a manner worthy of the Lord, to please Him in all respects, bearing fruit in every good work and increasing in the knowledge of God; strengthened with all power, according to His glorious might"* (Colossians 1:9-11). Consequently, it is our hope that we will, in service to the Father, continue to lead you closer to the Lord as we share those things we have heard from Him.

By His Grace,
Russell Raia, Jr. and Gina Raia

INTRODUCTION

So you think you know God? You believe you are saved and you are going to spend eternity in heaven with Jesus. Think again! You may not know God as well as you think. In fact, you may not know Him at all. It depends on what you believe, what you have been taught and whether you have a personal history with Him. Much of what a man believes about God is what He has been taught about God. If he has been taught wrongly, he knows God wrongly. Regardless of how sincerely he believes, what he believes may not be true.

This book is an account of our experience in coming to know the truth of the Lord; to truly know the Lord. It required a lot of unlearning and a lot of surrender. But it revealed to our hearts who God really is, what He is about, who we are and how what He is doing relates to us.

This book is a collection of some of the lessons we received from the Lord over the last twenty-eight years. All that is written is the result of a personal walk with the Lord. There is nothing presented herein that was learned by way of academics, nor should it be read in such manner. It is with confidence that we say, that unless the reader is prepared to have every ounce of his or her belief structure challenged, there is no reason to proceed. The words written hereafter are not written to any mere man. On the contrary, the words of this book are directed to the one who intends to fully submit himself without delay to the sanctifying work of the Holy Spirit and who understands that his life is the Lord's and not his own.

Our beliefs about who God is, who we are, what faith is, and what salvation is, were but a few of the things that were shattered when the Lord spoke to us the lessons shared in this book. It was terrifying and agonizing at first. Then understanding was followed by freedom. A God that we never knew before, suddenly became real to us. His words became our life's bread and every false belief was destroyed. We desire this experience for every man, although we realize not every man wants such an experience. It is our sincere hope that as you read these words that the Lord will grant to you the same revelation as has been granted to us; that you may know Him, the One true God.

For the sake of continuity, each lesson received is presented in a separate chapter in the order in which it was received. In some instances, later chapters build upon or rely upon that which was previously received. In other instances, the lesson stands alone. When reading text presented in the first person, it is presented by Russell Raia, Jr.

So as you begin this book, listen to what the Lord is saying; in your listening, learn Him; and in your learning Him, gain Life.

Table of Contents

Chapter 1

FAITH PERFECTED

Why Faith?

One evening as the church was meeting for prayer, my seventeen year-old son asked those gathered, "Why do we need faith when we have already seen God once?" There was complete silence in the room as everyone considered his question. After several moments, a comment or two was offered. The comments only seemed to reinforce the obvious; we had never considered that faith has an object, a goal, that when reached becomes greater than faith and faith would become secondary, essentially unnecessary. As I allowed my son's question to penetrate my soul, I realized that that single question, if answered by the Spirit of God, would propel each of us to the life of an overcomer.

A Means to an End

My son's question uncovered the work of faith in a believer. Faith is to lead to something else. Faith is not the end, but the means. Once the end is met, the means to the end is superseded. The means would have served its purpose.

This is not a unique concept to God. He proceeded the same way by introducing Christ into humanity by the giving of the Law. The Law was to reveal Christ (Galatians 3:24-25). Yet, once Christ was manifested, the Law was superseded by the very Object it was meant to reveal. Thereafter, any reliance upon the Law would work to nullify the Object of the Law for the one so relying.

The same divine method is seen with mercy. Mercy is given to all men by God without measure. Why? So man can see God and repent. Without mercy, judgment would overtake us and we would never know God. However, once we repent and by faith come to God, we are given grace. Grace is not that intangible, free, feel-good favor we so often speak of. That is descriptive of God's lovingkindness, not His Grace. Grace is nothing other than the power of God. It is the power that brings life to the dead. It is the power that sustains the weary. It is the power that keeps one from sin. Once redeemed, we are supplied grace by which to live a life pleasing to the Father. Without His grace (power) that life cannot be lived. Why? Because that life is not from this world; that life is from above. Furthermore, grace is not in the least bit free. In order to obtain it, you must pay for it with your entire life. You completely surrender yourself to God; He supplies you with power; resurrection power. You don't surrender, you don't receive grace. In other words, mercy is given to the unrepentant sinner; grace to the redeemed.

Once you are living a life by grace, mercy is done away with. Mercy led you to grace. Grace then propels you onward to all that are the intentions of God for humanity. If, having seen Christ, you then continue to live by mercy and not grace, you are likened to the one who would be circumcised in the flesh after having received Christ. Paul would tell you that Christ is no longer a benefit to you (Galatians 5:2).

So, just as the Law revealed Christ and mercy prepared the way for grace, faith is to introduce something else. My son's question suggested that upon seeing God once, faith should be secondary. Now faith is for things not seen. Faith is confidence in things unknown. So if my faith has brought me to see God, has my faith served its purpose?

The Challenge

What was common among all who heard the question posed by my son was that we each had personal experiences with the Lord. Now we were being challenged to look into those personal experiences and find the product of our faith. Was it external and temporal as is so often the case? Or was it eternal? Since I had been an eyewitness to most of the individual experiences gathered in the room that evening I can with confidence state that each of our individual experiences were such that not only had we received a temporal result from the Lord, but even more, we had seen the Lord, knew the reality of His presence and the truth of His faithfulness. That individual knowledge was for each of us, undeniable and could not be taken from us. Our faith in the Lord led us to see Him. As it pertained to the question posed by my son, the means led to the end. Why then were there still times in our lives of needing faith? What did we need faith for? Did we need faith to believe in a still unseen or unknown God? Or is the end to which faith is working in us more than just seeing or knowing God?

The End of Faith

The answer is found in the example of Jesus Himself. In his letter to the Philippians Paul says,

"That although He existed in the form of God, Jesus did not regard equality with God a thing to be grasped, but emptied Himself, taking the form of a bond-servant, and being made in the likeness of men. Being found in appearance as a man, He humbled Himself by becoming obedient to the point of death, even death on a cross" (Philippians. 2:6-8).

First, Jesus did not walk this earth in His own unique divinity. It is clear that before being found in appearance as a man, He emptied Himself of what was uniquely His; His place with the Almighty, before the foundations of the world. Second, He humbled Himself. This humbling was to His Father. Since He emptied Himself of His own unique divinity, He would have to trust in His Father for everything during His life as a man. As a man, He placed His faith in His God. This faith led Him to see, not as from divinity, but as from humanity. He saw His Father from earth. But was that the work of faith in Jesus? No. The work of faith was much more that seeing the Father. It was to be that as a result of that seeing the Father Jesus became obedient, even to the point of death. Faith had in Jesus its perfect result; obedience. It was faith perfected.

Our faith in God is intended to lead us to the place of obedience. If obedience is never reached, faith never reaches its end. Faith is never perfected. By reason of His obedience, "*God highly exalted Him, and bestowed on Him the name which is above every name, so that at the name of Jesus EVERY KNEE WILL BOW, of those who are in heaven and on earth and under the earth, and that every tongue will confess that Jesus Christ is Lord, to the glory of God the Father*" (Philippians 2:10-11).

Faith Perfected

The Law was given so that something greater could come. Mercy is poured out so that something greater can be received. Faith is sown so that something greater can be reaped.

On this particular evening as our church gathered to wait upon the Lord, His response was to challenge our understanding. He did so by shining a light on our beliefs and then asking us some very hard questions. Questions like, "Is your faith an end in itself or has it produced something greater?" We were forced to examine whether our faith in Him had led us to obedience in all things; to assess whether our faith had brought us to say that we can only do what we see the Father doing (John 5:19) or only say what we hear the Father saying (John 8:26).

Is my faith in God such that my food is to do the will of my Father (John 4:34)? When faith has its perfect way in us and our way is one of obedience to the Lord, faith will no longer be necessary and our life will be that of an overcomer.

Chapter 2

GOD IS *NOT* OBLIGATED TO ACCEPT YOU OR YOUR OFFERING

The Standard

Scripture Readings:

"And being found in appearance as a man, He humbled Himself by becoming obedient to death— even death on a cross! Therefore God exalted Him to the highest place and gave Him the name that is above every name" (Philippians 2:8-9).

"Consider it all joy, my brethren, when you encounter various trials, knowing that the testing of your faith produces endurance. And let endurance have its perfect result, so that you may be perfect and complete, lacking in nothing" (James 1:2-4).

"And do not be conformed to this world, but be transformed by the renewing of your mind, so that you may prove what the will of God is, that which is good and acceptable and perfect" (Romans 12:2).

"Now if perfection was through the Levitical priesthood (for on the basis of it the people received the Law), what further need was there for another priest to arise according to the order of Melchizedek, and not be designated according to the order of Aaron"(Hebrews 7:11)?

"[F]ixing our eyes on Jesus, the author and perfecter of faith, who for the joy set before Him endured the cross, despising the shame, and has sat down at the right hand of the throne of God" (Hebrews 12:2).

"Therefore, you are to be perfect, as your heavenly Father is perfect" (Matthew. 5:48).

"Oh, that one of you would shut the temple doors, so that you would not light useless fires on my altar! I am not pleased with you," says the LORD Almighty, "and I will accept no offering from your hands" (Malachi 1:10).

God only accepts perfection. We really need to understand that. He has no obligation to anyone, including Himself, to accept anything less than perfection. The problem is that it is a part of our sinful human nature to believe that less than perfect is acceptable to God. We have a deep-seeded belief that God will accept whatever we offer Him; something less than what He demands. But, He does not.

This deep-seeded belief stems from our wrong understanding of God and His ways. Christianity has taught that man can come to Jesus in whatever condition man finds himself, and the Lord will lovingly accept him. This is a lie and that lie has made inroads into every facet of our existence and has led far too many to worship a God who does not exist. It is not that God does not exist. Just not the God that Christianity has depicted.

The Word of God is clear, although understanding it requires spiritual sight. The Word makes clear that the Lord will find you in a fallen condition, "*for all have sinned and fall short of the glory of God*" (Romans 3:23). But just because He finds you in that condition, does not imply that you can come to Him and He will accept you, unless you present yourself as an acceptable offering, a perfect offering. This can only be accomplished by dying to self and surrendering all to Him.   Anything less is unacceptable to Him, and He is not bound to receive you.

We find two examples of this truth in the experiences of the rich young ruler and Nicodemus. In the case of the rich young ruler, Luke 18 reveals that the Lord found the young man, who then asked Jesus what was necessary to inherit eternal life. The Lord replied,

> "*You know the commandments, 'DO NOT COMMIT ADULTERY, DO NOT MURDER, DO NOT STEAL, DO NOT BEAR FALSE WITNESS, HONOR YOUR FATHER AND MOTHER.'*" **21** *And he said, "All these things I have kept from my youth."* **22** *When Jesus heard this, He said to him, "**One thing you still lack**; sell all that you possess and distribute it to the poor, and you shall have treasure in heaven; and come, follow Me."* [Bold emphasis added].

The Divine standard is directly before us. Perfection is required. The young man still lacked **one thing** *before* he could follow after Jesus. He needed to surrender all. He could not, so he left and he was not acceptable to God and God was not acceptable to him.

In the case of Nicodemus, the Lord said, *"Unless one is born again he cannot see the kingdom of God...and, unless one is born of water and the Spirit he cannot enter into the kingdom of God"* (John 3:3, 5). In other words, the Lord tells Nicodemus, "I have found you in the state of sinfulness and separation from God. Nevertheless, now you must be transformed in order to enter into My kingdom and see God. There is no other way." I have paraphrased John 3:1-8 here to illustrate the requirement of perfection for entrance into the kingdom of God. Nicodemus was completely unaware that he was lacking what was necessary to see the kingdom of God. Upon hearing God's standard, his only response to Jesus was, *"How can these things be?"* And Jesus replied, *"And you are the teacher of Israel..."*(John 3:9-10)?

The same truth is seen again and again, in the inverse, in each instance of a person becoming a disciple of Christ. In every case, the disciple left all to follow. They left all immediately and followed after the Lord. Consider the offerings of Peter, James, John, the woman with the issue of blood, the Roman centurion, Moses, Paul, Abraham, Elisha, Jeremiah and others. Everyone who comes into the kingdom of God does so by way of offering to God a perfect offering of himself. The same requirement is upon us in our day. Neither God nor His ways have changed.

God Is Not a Man

Christianity's evangelistic tag line, "that all can come to Jesus just the way you are and He will accept you" has morphed into a religious doctrine that allows for God's standards to be disregarded and man's lusts to flourish. It is clear, that without Jesus, man has no hope. It is He, the Son of God, who makes perfect that which is imperfect. But that perfection is not present in us unless that perfection is coming out of us and returning to God. The work of the cross must bear fruit in us or that work was in vain. For you will be known by your fruit. Consider the Apostle Paul's heart felt plea to the churches of Galatia. Note, that Paul is writing to churches and the message he delivers is, "the work of the cross is in vain unless and until Christ (perfection) is formed in you" (see Galatians 4:1-20).

As stated previously, this ignorance about God and His ways has extended into every facet of our existence, including the worship of God Himself. We evidence our worship of Him through our many and various offerings. Those offerings come from every corner of our life. They could be our time, our thoughts, our talents, the fruits of our labor, or any such thing. We present to God these various offerings as a sign of our worship, believing He has accepted our offering and He is satisfied. But the truth is He has established what is acceptable and what is unacceptable and He will not receive that which is unacceptable.

However, we do not pay attention to His standard. We are satisfied with offering Him what *we want* to give and believe He should be and will be pleased with whatever we give. We even go so far as to applaud a well meant intention and reward a good effort that falls short of His mark. In light of His previously stated standard, His response to our misplaced effort is and will be, "That is not going to work."

We see very clearly in the life of King Saul that he believed offering God less than perfect would be satisfactory. King Saul was commanded by God through the Prophet Samuel to attack and totally destroy the Amalekites. At the conclusion of the battle, Saul and his men spared the Amalekite king and gathered all that was considered valuable and worthy as spoil from the battle. Part of that spoil was sacrificed to God as a worship offering. Saul was confronted by the Prophet about his disobedience as recorded in 1 Samuel 15. Although King Saul was adamant that he did according to the Lord's command, he was stripped of the throne because of his less than perfect obedience. Regardless of his intention or motive, his offering was completely unacceptable to God.

It is a human trait to do "a thing," any "thing." But God is not interested in a "thing." He would rather receive nothing, than get something He did not ask for or command. We make God out to be a man. God is not a man. He wants the thing that means something. He wants the thing that counts. He wants the perfect offering; true surrender; true obedience. Otherwise, He will not accept it.

But What About God's Love

The Word of God establishes God's standard. It is what it is. This is what He is going to accept. He is not going to take anything less and we are made aware of this in advance. Yet, because we are not willing to obey the Lord, we give Him less than that standard. In the moment we give it to Him, He may not say anything about it. He does not say, "thank you" or "this stinks." Nevertheless, He does not accept it because He cannot. He will not accept anything but perfection. Just because we do not have an immediate response from God expressing His displeasure with our gift, does not mean that we are not guilty of presenting a worthless offering. He has set His standard. We are not meeting His standard.

Most Christians would flatly deny that they offer less than a perfect offering to God. In their estimation, their offering is exactly what is required of them. As with the rich young ruler and Nicodemus discussed above, we are more satisfied with ourselves and with others than is God. For example, our standard is to know and keep all of the commandments. Today, you are considered "spiritual" or at least not worldly if you even know the commandments of the Lord, much less keep them. Yet, today, as with the rich young ruler, knowing and keeping the commandments is not satisfactory to God if He requires more.

The danger in all of this is that when we are in error, we are the last to see our wrong. Our flesh, being alive and well, prevents us from recognizing our sin. But God is merciful to continue to reveal to us the error of our ways. Despite our denials of wrongdoing, the clearest evidence that we are at odds with God on this matter is found in our willingness to accept from others less than what God commands of them. Jesus never altered the standard of His Father so as to appease any man. He continually presented the requirements of God and you either accepted it by way of your repentance or rejected it and went your way.

God commands that we give all of our self. This total surrender is _the_ necessary offering to be made if one is to be considered to be in the body of Christ. Yet, Christianity rejects this standard and sets its own standard, by expecting and accepting less from people, resulting in a church populace that is far from acceptable to God. Because we are willing to accept from each other less than what God commands, our churches and fellowships are filled with King Sauls, rich young rulers and Nicodemuses. But you know what? God does not work that way. God does not include you in His fellowship of eternal life if you give Him less than perfect. That is where we differ from God. We are lenient where He is not. We are accepting when He is not.

As I shared God's standard of perfection recently, I was questioned about the love of God. "Does not His love cover our shortcomings? Will not His love overtake my imperfections?" My response was, "this has nothing to do with love. This has to do with obedience." As Christians, we have this tendency to proclaim God's love as the answer to all of our shortcomings. The reality is that God loves everybody, yet most of us will be cast away from His presence (Matthew 7:23). Does not the Scripture state that, "God so loved the *world* .... and... while we were yet *sinners*, Christ died for us" (John 3:16; Romans 5:8)? God does not love "His people" only. God loves everybody, before and after they were born, or born again. But that love does not mean that He accepts less than perfection.

Do you think when He was speaking to Moses in the burning bush that He did not have love for the sons of Israel who were back in Egypt? He told Moses, "*I hear the cry of My people*" (Exodus 3:7). God's heart went out to them. Did that mean because of His love and what He purposed to do through Moses that He would accept less than perfect? Well, just go 45 years into their future and you will find out. No, absolutely not! He will never accept less and that had nothing to do with love. But because we do not know or understand God, we offer Him less and we are also willing to accept less from each other and we should not.

We should however, through the Holy Spirit, be more like Peter when Ananias and Sapphira came with less than perfection. But we are not Peter, because their gift is acceptable to us. Why should we turn it down? Why should we reject it? If they gave it, we should accept it, right? The Apostle Paul, as well as Jude, addressed this tendency of tolerating less than perfection several times. In those instances, there were those who were part of the fellowship, part of the church. Paul identified them by name and Jude said they were men who are hidden within the body. The admonition from Paul and Jude to the churches was and is that they cannot count this as acceptable. The imperfection must be addressed.

What we fail to grasp in our reading of these accounts is that the churches they were addressing let the unacceptable remain for far too long. They were apparently unaware such conduct on their part was unacceptable to God. In 1 Corinthians 5, Paul is addressing a report that there was a young man who was guilty of sexual immortally within the assembly and the church failed to remove him from their midst. In other words, Paul was saying to the Corinthians, "you have accepted this. You ought to be ashamed of yourselves." Again, we are shown how we are more willing than God to accept less than perfection. Paul dealt with the immorality directly by handing the offender over to Satan and he rebuked the church for their arrogance and wickedness.

One-On-One With God

There is a prevalent and disturbing phenomenon that occurs within the Christian church. Christians love to gather and talk "about the Lord." Such meetings and celebrations are frequent and extended. The only problem is God is not in attendance at those gatherings. When He shows up to a gathering, He has on His mind to talk "about you and your condition." When that occurs, the seats empty and the meetings are short. We love to listen to messages about the life of Christ. We pride ourselves on knowing them so well. But no one is interested in Christ prying into our lives. Who is ever interested in being the subject matter of the message?

What person ever wants to be seated at the interrogation table?

Well, I recently found myself at that table being interrogated by the Lord with respect to accepting less than a perfect offering. It involved several people who were directed to be a part of our local body. It was understood by those involved that God had directed such persons to become a part of the church. Even though the Lord had spoken, their presence and participation in our gatherings was sporadic at best. Some days they would call saying they could not make it to our meeting. Other times they would simply not show up. I never said anything because I did not want to seem overbearing. I wanted to understand and love them. I would tell myself maybe they are just not ready. I believed that in time, they would come around. When they did attend our meetings the Lord ministered to them but that only resulted in their appearance at our meetings being even more infrequent.

After several months it advanced to the point where they informed me that they would no longer be attending church and would be looking to attend elsewhere. In the midst of this, they invited me and my family to join them for a time of games and fun. I explained that God had made His will clear and they were clearly telling Him they were not interested in obeying. They were however, very interested in living out their own desires and wishes.

The Lord revealed to me His displeasure with them and what was occurring. He told me that He did not accept their offering. What they were giving Him of their time and their life was what they wanted to give to Him, not what He commanded. In this instance, their offering would be to go to a church of their choosing, where they felt comfortable and loved, or to simply not go to church at all. The Lord kept saying to me, "Obedience is the only acceptable offering. I will not accept their sacrifice."

Now I was faced with a problem. Could I accept what God could not accept? Could I continue in the relationship as though no disobedience was occurring? The answer was no, I could not. I exhorted them to obey the Lord. Their response was not surprising, but nevertheless disappointing.

I am not sharing this experience to highlight a wrong in them, but in me. I was the one who was in the wrong. Not in regard to them, but in regard to God. I was enabling their sin by my willingness to accept from them what I knew to be disobedience. Instead of accepting their disobedience and making excuses for it, I should have from the beginning been more willing to call it unacceptable, and hold myself and them accountable to what God said. It may have only been several months before I obeyed, but it lasted too long as far as the Lord was concerned.

The Day of Decision

We are solemnly warned about the peril of unbelief in Hebrews 3. There we are reminded about all those who came out of Egypt led by Moses whose bodies fell in the wilderness because of their unbelief. On that day the Lord swore that they who were disobedient would not enter His rest (Hebrews 3:16-18). Today I encourage you not to be hardened by the deceitfulness of sin (Hebrews 3:13). Disobedience is the manifestation of unbelief. Giving to God a less than perfect offering is disobedience. Those who were led by Moses had the truth preached to them but failed to enter [His rest][His kingdom] because of disobedience.

> "*Today if you hear His voice,*
> *Do not harden your hearts*" (Hebrews 4:7).

What are you doing in your life that I have done in mine? God is not like me or you. God does not give less than perfect and He does not receive less than perfect. You have to understand it goes both directions with Him. Every good and perfect gift comes from Him. The gift that God received from Jesus was perfect. The gift that He gave to man was perfect. Because of our hardness of heart and our unwillingness to accept the truth, we believe that God accepts whatever we give Him. He does not, unless what we have given Him is perfect.

All that we have given Him that is imperfect, meaning not out of obedience but out of sacrifice, has been and will always be, unacceptable to Him. So you may get to heaven one day and expect to see a load of offerings that you have given Him and the unacceptable ones, according to the Gospel, will be burned up. They will no longer exist. Actually, they never did exist, but you did not know that. However, you should have because the Gospel tells you so. And now that you have finished this chapter you know so.

Chapter 3

To Know the Lord Is
To Know His Ways

Israel – The People of God

Exodus 3 -

13 Then Moses said to God, "Behold, I am going to the sons of Israel, and I will say to them, 'The God of your fathers has sent me to you.' Now they may say to me, 'What is His name?' What shall I say to them?" 14 God said to Moses, "I AM WHO I AM"; and He said, "Thus you shall say to the sons of Israel, 'I AM has sent me to you.'" 15 God, furthermore, said to Moses, "Thus you shall say to the sons of Israel, 'The LORD, the God of your fathers, the God of Abraham, the God of Isaac, and the God of Jacob, has sent me to you.' .... ¹⁸ *They will pay heed to what you say; and you with the elders of Israel will come to the king of Egypt and you will say to him, 'The LORD, the God of the Hebrews, has met with us. So now, please, let us go a three days' journey into the wilderness, that we may sacrifice to the LORD our God.'*

Unlike any other people, Israel was known among the nations as a people belonging to the Lord God of heaven. The relationship began when God called a man named Abram to leave his country and his father's house and travel to a place that he would be shown; a place that the Lord would give to him and where the Lord would bless him (Genesis 12:1-4). The relationship between God and the Hebrew people was unique. Although God had relationship with men prior to this time; men like Adam, Enoch, and Noah, never before had God established a relationship with an entire people. It was by and through this relationship that the Lord would deal with the entire human race.

We have the first glimpse of these dealings in Chapter 14 of Genesis when Abram went in pursuit of Chedorlaomer, king of Elam; Tidal, king of Goiim; Amraphel, king of Shinar; and Arioch, king of Ellasar, after they had captured Abram's nephew Lot and taken all of his possessions. Abram overtook the kings and defeated them, recovering his nephew along with his people and his possessions. After returning from the defeat of

Chedorlaomer and the kings who were with him, the king of Sodom went out to greet Abram at the valley of Shaveh, and Melchizedek, king of Salem brought out bread and wine and blessed Abram and said,

> "Blessed be Abram of God Most High, possessor of heaven and earth; and blessed be God Most High, Who has delivered your enemies into your hand" (Genesis 14:17-20).

This victory and the subsequent blessing was the first fulfillment of the promise made by God to Abram in Genesis, when God said to him,

> "And I will make you a great nation, and I will bless you, and make your name great; and so you shall be a blessing; and I will bless those who bless you, and the one who curses you I will curse. And in you all the families of the earth will be blessed" (Genesis 12:2-3).

In Chapter 37 of Genesis we see a continuation of this relationship between God and the sons of Israel. In this chapter, Joseph, the youngest son of his father Jacob, has a dream from God. The dream and its interpretation led to Joseph being sold into slavery by his brothers. Joseph is taken to Egypt where, after years of imprisonment and hardship, he rises to power, being second only to Pharaoh in all Egypt. Then through Joseph, God delivers the sons of Israel from sure death during a time of drought and famine, while at the same time blessing Egypt with provision and protection.

In the Book of Joshua we get yet another look at the relationship between God and Israel and how that relationship is acknowledged by the people around them. It has been nearly 500 years since the time of Joseph. The sons of Israel have lived in Egypt as slaves for 400 of those years. Now, in Chapter 2 of Joshua, Joshua is leading the sons of Israel across the Jordan and into the lands of the Amorites and Canaanites and towards the fortified city of Jericho, again in fulfillment of God's promise to Abram. From Shittim, Joshua sends two Hebrew spies into Jericho to search out the land. While the spies searched out Jericho, they came across a woman named Rahab. During their brief encounter with her, the following exchange occurred:

> "Now [Rahab] came up to them on the roof, and said to the men, "I know that the LORD has given you the land, and that the terror of you has fallen on us, and that all the inhabitants of the land have melted away before you. For we have heard how the LORD dried up the water of the Red Sea before you when you came out of Egypt, and what you did to the two kings of the Amorites who were beyond the Jordan, to Sihon and Og, whom you utterly destroyed. When we heard it, our hearts melted and no courage remained in any man any longer because of you; for the LORD your God, He is God in heaven above and on earth beneath" (Joshua. 2:8-11).

After reading these brief accounts of Israel's early history, it is evident God had established a special relationship with Israel. However, despite such manifestations of favor and power on their behalf, the relationship that the sons of Israel had with the Lord God was not what it should have been. Despite all that God did for Israel, the Hebrew people lacked a true knowledge of Him. It does not take much digging into the history of this people to conclude that, in reality, they knew the Lord God of heaven no more than the heathen nations around them.

For generations they were the beneficiaries of God's grace and loving-kindness, yet their refusal to surrender to Him and to obey His commandments led to their repeated servitude (see Judges 2:2-3; 3:7-8; 3:12-14; 4:1-3; 6:1-2; 10:6-9). They knew the acts of the God of heaven. They saw frequently the work of His hand, but except for a small minority, the sons of Israel did not know Him. Psalm 103:7 states, *"He made known His ways to Moses, His acts to the sons of Israel."* There is a great difference between knowing the Lord and having Him act on your behalf. To know the Lord is to know the ways of the Lord. Apart from knowing His ways, at best you will be a beneficiary of His acts, but your experience of Him is from afar. You know of Him, but you do not know Him. It was because of their lack of knowing Him that most of Israel perished on their way to the land of promise (see Hebrews 3:16-19).

Not unlike Israel, the church sees much of the hand of God, but knows little of His ways. A truthful analysis of the state of the church would suggest that it is *only* His hand that they seek, despite the assertions to the contrary. Because of the ignorance to God's ways, many fail to come to a true knowledge of Him. They have been sold on a God of blessing and favor and are addicted to as much of Him as they can get. In the Letter to the Hebrews, the church is warned against falling victim to the same sin of unbelief and disobedience that Israel fell into in the wilderness (Hebrews 3:12-19; 4:1-3).

If the church is to survive in this day; if it is to avoid the wrath and judgment of God, it must come to the place of knowing the ways of God. To know the ways of God is to move away from a carnal "spiritual" life; a spiritual life set on advancing the desires of the flesh (Philippians. 3:17-19); a spiritual life that sees God as one who gives us all that we can ask or think (Luke 9:51-56). To know the ways of the Lord is to present yourself as a living and holy sacrifice, acceptable to Him (Romans 12:1).

God's ways are many, but His ways are unchanging. It is necessary for us to come to an understanding of God's ways so that we may know Him. His ways are always *"living and active"* and *"piercing as far as the division of soul and spirit," ..., judging the thoughts and intentions of the heart* (Hebrews 4:12). His ways are not always what we want, but they are what we need. Regardless of the cost, it is far better to know the Lord and His ways, than to simply know His acts.

It Is His Way to
Always Address Our Sin

One of the principal ways of the Lord is that He is always addressing our sinful condition. He is always convicting, purging, and purifying. This is far removed from the God that pours out "blessings" on His children.

As Christians, we think we have something in relation to God, but He is always quick to point out that we are not there. He is always challenging our ground of spiritual contentment. Few people professing a faith in Christ recognize God's way concerning man's sinful condition. This is due in part to a misunderstanding of the forgiveness of sin. The forgiveness of sin is an action of God; it is what God has done for us, through the work of the cross. However, our continuing sinful condition is not related to any action of God or a lack of forgiveness, but a lack of repentance. Repentance is an action of man. It is a responsibility of man, not God. Unless man repents of his evil way he remains alienated from God, despite the work of the cross. It is this kind of failure in understanding God's ways that keeps us in a place of judgment and separation in relationship to God.

The ways of God are at work always and toward all men. If there was anyone who could think he had something in relation to God or take any stock in whom and where he was with the Lord, it would be Joshua, son of Nun. He succeeded Moses in leading Israel into the land of promise and he was given the privilege of being the first to taste the gift given to Abraham by marching the sons of Israel in conquest of Jericho. It was in that environment that the Lord addresses Joshua and his sinful condition. In Chapter 5 of Joshua we read the following,

"Now it came about when Joshua was by Jericho, that he lifted up his eyes and looked, and behold, a man was standing opposite him with his sword drawn in his

hand, and Joshua went to him and said to him, 'Are you for us or for our adversaries?' He said, 'No; rather I indeed come now as captain of the host of the LORD.' And Joshua fell on his face to the earth, and bowed down, and said to him, 'What has my lord to say to his servant?' The captain of the LORD'S host said to Joshua, 'Remove your sandals from your feet, for the place where you are standing is holy.' And Joshua did so" (Joshua 5:13-15).

Joshua's initial question to the man standing before him reveals his ground of spiritual contentment. Joshua believed he had something or was someone in regard to the Lord. He asks, *"Are you for us or for our adversaries?"* This statement is made on the ground or assumption that, "we are the people of the Living God and as far as I [Joshua] know, you are not. You had better state your intention or else you will surely die." The man replies, "No; I'm in charge here Joshua, not you." Immediately Joshua changes his position (repents) which is evidenced by his falling face down to the ground and bowing down. However, his positional change was not complete. He is then further purged and purified when the captain of the Lord's host commands Joshua to remove his sandals from his feet because he was standing on holy ground. Again, Joshua repented, as evidenced by his obedience to the command.

We must recognize that Joshua's spiritual position at the beginning of his encounter with the captain of the host of the Lord was far different than his position at the end of the encounter. At the beginning Joshua is conducting himself as one would expect from a natural point of view. He *is* the military and governing leader of the Hebrew people and it is foreseeable that Joshua would confront an unknown or possibly hostile party. Be that as it may, he was not conducting himself as God would have it. Joshua was unaware of who was before him and unaware of where he stood. From the beginning it was the intent and purpose of the Lord to bring Joshua to a new position. At the end of his encounter with the captain of the host of the Lord, Joshua is repentant (humble), both physically and spiritually. It was the way of the Lord to address Joshua's wrong position (sinful condition). In other words, the Lord was showing to Joshua and revealing to us, that his ground of spiritual contentment had blinded him to his spiritual condition and to the holiness and presence of God.

Man has a strong tendency to find a place of spiritual contentment. It is this tendency that finds religion so appealing. God challenges our spiritual ground and is always working to bring us to the place of spiritual discontentment. He does this by revealing Himself and allowing us to see ourselves in relation to Him and His holiness. The Lord operates this way with all men as we can see in the lives of the rich young ruler (Luke 18:18-27) (righteousness through the law), Nicodemus (relationship with God through natural birthright) (John 3:1-10), and the woman at the well (finding earthly value in being a descendant of Jacob) (John 4:7-26). And I think we are all familiar with the spiritual contentment that Peter was grounded on when he declared to the Lord that he would not allow any harm to come to Him (Matthew 16:17-19; 21-23).

Certainly, these are not the only instances where the Lord is showing us that we hold one position with Him and He holds another. But, these examples provide us with insight as to the way of the Lord. Again, it is His way to continually address our sinful nature. If we remain unaware that this is His way, and continue to hold to the belief that we are "His people" whom He will forever bless, we will never repent of our condition, therefore, never departing from our sinfulness and separation from Him. We will never know Him and He will never know us.

Slowness Is His Way

"Blessed is he who does not take offense at Me" (Luke 7:23).

Oh, the blessings found in not being offended at God. During one of our church services, the Lord sang to us the following:

> *Follow. I will lead.*
> *Slow down. I will lead.*

The lines repeated a number of times as the Lord conveyed His will to us. It was not by accident that the Lord sang what He did, because more often than not our offense at God is related to our lack of understanding of His slowness.

Slowness is part of the character of God. It always has been and always will be. When you do not understand this, then you will become more offended as your life goes on. God has never been quick about anything; that is just His nature. His slowness is an attribute of His mercy. It is the attribute of the Divine nature that allows for repentance in place of judgment.

I cannot tell you what a blessing it is to understand that God's slowness is what allows us to obtain salvation (2 Peter 3:15). We have no justification before the Lord in our unrighteousness; therefore He is justified in an immediate execution of His judgment. But it is His character, the attribute that we are discussing here that allows for repentance and ultimately salvation. He does not just want us to benefit from that character attribute; He wants us to become that character attribute.

One example of Divine slowness is found in the life and ministry of Noah.   For nearly one hundred years he built a boat and preached the message of righteousness. In those one hundred years, nothing changed. Not one soul responded to the call of the Lord to repentance. Yet, Noah never faltered. Noah never became angry with God or offended at his calling. There was nothing quick or externally rewarding about what Noah was commanded to do. He did it nonetheless. Noah understood Divine slowness and became divine slowness. If you found yourself in Noah's position today, how many opportunities do you think you could come up with in one hundred years to be offended at God for His slowness?

We get offended with God if hundred minutes pass and we think something should happen but, does not happen. Forty years in the wilderness and what really changed? Nothing changed. Divine slowness! The God that we call Father is a slow God. He desires for that divine attribute of slowness to be found in us. Not only to show that we know Him and would not be offended at Him, but that we would be like Him.

The Lord does not want us to be offended at Him, but He does not change Himself so that we will not be. God brings men into situations that allow them to trust and know Him. This is accomplished during times of slowness. This slowness is subjective, meaning the "delay" may be minutes, hours, or years. Nevertheless, the delay is beyond your individual expectation of God's timely intervention into your situation. Most often, what are born in these times of slowness are fear, anxiety and offense, and not trust.

One such opportunity was presented to Mary and Martha when they sent word to Jesus that their brother Lazarus was sick. God delayed Jesus' arrival. Not to harm Lazarus or his sisters, but to bring glory to God through his resurrection. The sisters' offense at God's slowness is seen in their words to Jesus, "*Lord, my brother would not have died if...*" (John 11:21, 32).

Another opportunity to know God and His slowness is found with Jairus as recorded in Luke 8. There, Jairus fell at the feet of Jesus, imploring Him to come to his house and heal his dying daughter. As they went, Jesus was "Divinely" delayed by a woman in need of a healing. Jesus stopped and ministered to her while Jairus watched and waited. While the Lord was still speaking to the woman, someone from the house of Jairus came saying that his daughter had died. Upon hearing this, Jesus turned to Jairus and said, "*Do not be afraid any longer; only believe, and she will be made well*" (Luke 8:50). Jesus and Jairus then proceeded to his house. Shortly thereafter, Jesus took the young girl by the hand and her life returned to her. Jairus in this instance, by not being offended at God, came to know God and the attribute of His slowness and came to experience the faithfulness of God and the healing and restoration of his child.

Probably the saddest example of delay is seen with John the Baptist (see Luke 7:18-23). Finding himself in prison, John had plenty of time to ponder all that he was expecting of God after the revealing of the Christ. It is obvious from his question to Jesus, *"Are You the Expected One or do we look for someone else?"* that the slowness of God was not having its way with John. Jesus, knowing the condition of John's heart and the effect of that condition, pointed out to him that the Scripture was being fulfilled and blessed is the one who is not offended by God's way. John's offense, led to distrust which led to blindness which leads to death. Blessed is the one who is *not* offended.

There are countless more times in the Bible, where men are placed into circumstances, situations, and conditions that produce a need for the Lord to intervene. The circumstances, situations, and conditions, usually produce in us petitions of prayer; petitions to the Lord for Him to do something; to bring about a resolution or an end to something or just give an answer. What happens when He does not answer that prayer is that we become offended. That offense does not have to be anything bigger than a sliver in your heart, but it has done its work. The sliver of offense has given birth to distrust. That distrust eats away at hope and it disables your ability to endure. You may trust Him more than you do not trust Him, but you do not trust Him completely. All of this is the result of not understanding the ways of God.

And It Goes On and On

There is not enough time or room in this chapter to cover all of the ways of the Lord. Again, there are limitless ways of the Lord. We have touched on a few here. In the next chapter, *"The War of the Lord"* we discuss the way of the Lord as it concerns Satan. And in the first chapter, *"Faith Perfected"* we discussed the way of the Lord concerning trials and tribulations.

The sons of Israel were a people chosen to be a people for God's own pleasure; to be a people who would know, love and worship the Lord. Sadly, the sons of Israel squandered that opportunity. Today, we are in danger of doing the same thing. If we remain content with knowing God from afar; if we want to receive only the "benefits" of being called "His child" and show no interest in truly knowing Him, we will have the same results. We too will be laid low in the wilderness. We too will fall under the mighty hand of God before we see the land of promise. Determine in your heart today to seek to know the Lord by knowing His ways. Then, not only know His ways, but love His ways, and by doing so, love Him.

✛

Chapter 4

THE WAR OF THE LORD

The One Who Contends
With God

Then the Lord said to Job, *"Will the faultfinder contend with the Almighty? Let him who reproves God answer it."* Then Job answered the Lord and said, *"Behold, I am insignificant; what can I reply to You? I lay my hand on my mouth. Once I have spoken, and I will not answer; even twice, and I will add nothing more"* (Job 40:2-5).

For centuries Job has been characterized as representing the suffering of the innocent at the hand of evil. He is commonly portrayed as being the victim of a heavenly contest between God and Satan. However, this is not scripturally correct, not even within the text of the book itself. Certainly Job endured with patience, but it was not at the hand of the devil, but at the hand of the Lord. James confirms to us that in the person of Job we *"have seen the outcome of the Lord's dealings, that the Lord is full of compassion and is merciful"* (James 5:11).

First, it was the Lord's dealings, not Satan's. Satan was the instrument the Lord used, but it was the Lord's dealings with Job. Likewise with us, it will always be the Lord's dealings. The traditional Christian teaching is that Satan attacked righteous Job. Read again, Job 1:6-12. It is God, not Satan, who first brings up the name of Job. Further, Satan is instructed by God as to what he can and cannot do regarding Job (Job 1:12; 2:6). Satan, as an instrument of the Lord, must and does obey.

Second, the Lord was compassionate and merciful because that is what Job needed to bring him to the place of repentance and escape God's judgment (Job 42:5-6). What many fail to see in the Book of Job is that God had a plan. God had a purpose to fulfill. It was to bring Job to a place where he was not. God had dealings to have with Job and He had them. The account illustrated in Job is not one of Satan, "God's enemy and man's nemesis," seeking to destroy someone esteemed by the Lord. For one thing, Satan is not the antagonist. He is not the enemy of God, nor is he the enemy of Job. As a matter of fact, after Job 2:8, we never hear of or from Satan again. Who is ultimately dealt with in the book is not Satan, but Job. And after Job finally repents in Chapter 42, the Lord makes a point to rebuke Job's friends but says nothing to Satan.

Identifying the Enemy

The Book of Job is for us a beginner's handbook on relationships. It really needs to be the first book we read when we pick up the Bible, because in it we discover the relationships between: God and Satan; God and Man; Man and Satan; and Man and Man. If these relationships are not properly understood, confusion and error result. The present state of Christianity is the proof. Because there is ignorance as to these relationships many have not understood God's dealings with man as recorded in the Bible.

The Book of Judges alone illustrates how God is purposed to bring an obstinate people to have complete faith in Him and how He employs "the enemy" to facilitate His purpose (see Judges 2:14; 3:7-8, 12-14; 4:1-3; 6:1-2; 10:6-8; 13:1). We have likewise not understood God's dealings with us today. We take stock in calling ourselves God's children, but we ignorantly rebuke Him when He comes to us in trials and tribulations. Recall the words of the prophet Jeremiah to the inhabitants of Jerusalem, *"It will be, that the nation or the kingdom which will not serve him, Nebuchadnezzar king of Babylon, and which will not put its neck under the yoke of the king of Babylon, I will punish that nation with the sword, with famine and with pestilence," declares the Lord, "until I have destroyed it by his hand. "Bring your necks under the yoke of the king of Babylon and serve him and his people, and live"* (Jeremiah 27:8, 12)! Since Satan is an instrument of the Lord, all of our "rebuking" and "casting out" in the name of the Lord is foolishness and hardness of heart. It is the Lord who has directed the "strong man" to his mission; a mission to accomplish the Lord's purpose in us.

Our ignorance of who the Lord is and how He works is further explained in the following quote by Sūn Wu, better known as Sun Tzu, an ancient Chinese military general, strategist, and philosopher from the Zhou Dynasty. Sun Tzu said in his book *The Art of War*, "If you know the enemy and know yourself, you need not fear the result of a hundred battles. If you know yourself but not the enemy, for every victory gained you will also suffer a defeat. If you know neither the enemy nor yourself, you will succumb in every battle."[1]

The evidence is overwhelming. We have to look no further than our own life experience. It is either littered with defeats, or whatever victories we may have experienced are extinguished by an equal number of setbacks. The reason – we do not know ourselves or our enemy. So in Job, we should and need to come to see who God is, who we are, and who Satan is.

As to man (Job), Satan is the hand of God causing trials for the purposes of "*bringing to light the things hidden in the darkness and disclose the motives of men's hearts*" (1 Corinthians 4:5). As to God, Satan is the smith who blows the fire of coals, or the destroyer who brings ruin (Isaiah 54:16). In each and every case, he is directed by God and operates within the given directive. We also see this truth in God's use of the Assyrians and the Babylonians as well as others to bring trials, tribulations and judgments to His people (Isaiah 8:1-4; Jeremiah 22:6-7).

As to God, man is an unknowingly separated and antagonistic mortal and needs to be brought near. As to man, man without God (Job's three friends) is the blind leading the blind. As to man; man with God (Jesus) is the image of the invisible God.

As the Scripture verse at the head of this chapter suggests, the Lord was contending with Job. If you are one who believes that God was pleased with Job and that it was Satan who was the enemy to be dealt with, it is suggested that you reconsider your theology after reading what God had to say to Job after listening to thirty chapters of words without knowledge: Then the Lord answered Job out of the storm and said,

"Now gird up your loins like a man; I will ask you, and you instruct Me. Will you really annul My judgment? Will you condemn Me that you may be justified? Or do you have an arm like God, and can you thunder with a voice like His? Adorn yourself with eminence and dignity, and clothe yourself with honor and majesty. Pour out the overflowings of your anger, and look on everyone who is proud, and make him low. Look on everyone who is proud, and humble him, and tread down the wicked where they stand. Hide them in the dust together; bind them in the hidden place. Then I will also confess to you, that your own right hand can save you" (Job 40:6-14).

Uncovering the Real Enemy

The Lord was purposed to work something out of Job that Job could not recognize. It is something terrible, something evil, something God is unceasingly at war with.

What was known to the Lord, but hidden from Job was his self-awareness. It was an awareness that caused Job's eyes to turn upon self; an awareness that brought up defenses and justifications. Job's self-awareness brought to life, the self-life of Job. It was a hidden evil brought to light by the mercies of God through difficult circumstances.

This self-life is determined to exist apart and independent from God. It is this self-life that prompts Job to demand from the Lord an answer for his sufferings (Job 10:1-7). It is this self-life that moves Job to presume that God owes him an explanation (Job 23:1-6). This awareness at first glance may not even seem out-of-line, much less an evil, but to God it is the worst of all evils. Self-awareness is the root that produces pride as its fruit. It is His foremost enemy and He will contend with it from generation to generation. (1 Peter 5:5).

One of the reasons this evil was hidden from Job was religion. Job prayed and he offered burnt offering. He feared God and turned away from evil. But did that mean he was in right standing with God? From God's dealings with him, it appears not. Religion, Christianity not excepted, is the human disease whose root is self-awareness. Religion had its beginnings in the Garden of Eden when Adam and Eve made for themselves coverings with fig leaves after they had become aware of their own nakedness (Genesis 3:7). It is the same evil that raises its head again within Judaism when Jesus comes. The pride of the Pharisees is the fruit of their self-awareness. Even the Samaritan woman at the well, aware of her heritage in Jacob, is at first blind to the One who can give her Living

Water. Self-awareness causes one to look not upon God, but upon oneself. It blinds with pride. Pride was hidden in Job's heart.

The Beginnings of Evil

Such evil did not originate with Job. Self-awareness first reared its ugly head in heaven. Now self-awareness is not something that was created, but it is a choice available within the universe of freewill. God gave freewill. In each and every circumstance, good or bad, one having freewill can choose to look to God (the Giver or Creator); or to look upon themselves.

Traditionally, Satan is seen as an envious and rebellious angel, determined to overthrow God. Some even view him as a god of evil. But, God did not create a devil. Nor, did God create an evil god. No, the Biblical account of Lucifer's beginning is far different. Ezekiel 28:12-15 records the Lord speaking thusly,

"You had the seal of perfection, full of wisdom and perfect in beauty. You were in Eden, the garden of God; every precious stone was your covering: the ruby, the topaz and the diamond; the beryl, the onyx and the jasper; the lapis lazuli, the turquoise and the emerald; and the gold, the workmanship of your settings and sockets, was in you. On the day that you were created they were prepared. You were the anointed cherub who covers, and I placed you there. You were on the holy mountain of God; you walked in the midst of the stones

of fire. You were blameless in your ways from the day you were created."

However, such a perfect and anointed work of the Lord, something He brought so near to Himself, was overcome by an evil as seemingly harmless as self-awareness. Lucifer looked upon what God had made and became self-aware, prideful. Ezekiel 28: 17 says, *"Your heart was lifted up because of your beauty; you corrupted your wisdom by reason of your splendor."* Violence (self-awareness) internally filled Lucifer and he sinned. Pride was produced by his self-awareness and he declared, *"I will ascend to heaven, I will raise my throne above the stars of God and I will make myself like the Most High God"* (Isaiah 14:13-14). As a result of Lucifer's sin God pronounced an eternal judgment against him and declared war against all that is evil and all that would raise itself against the Lord (Ezekiel 28:16). God declared war on something greater than Lucifer, something far more evil than the devil, something that made even Lucifer its victim. It was this violent evil that was found in the anointed cherub. It was this corruption that caused this one who was on the holy mountain of God, walked in the midst of the stones of fire and blameless in his ways to sin against the Lord (Ezekiel 28:14-15, 17). It was this eternal disease that was now within man and it was this that God sent His Son to destroy.

The End of Evil

And destroy it He has. Jesus overcame self-awareness. No pride ever entered His heart. Even before He came to earth as a child He was exercising dominion over self-awareness. According to Philippians 2:6-7, "*Christ Jesus, who, although He existed in the form of God, did not regard equality with God a thing to be grasped, but emptied Himself, taking the form of a bond-servant, and being made in the likeness of men.*" In heaven with the Father, Jesus had the opportunity to look upon Himself and who He was and say no. But He did not. He never took His eyes off of His God. If going to earth is what the Father wanted, so be it. Self-awareness was defeated with humility, love and faith in the one true God.

Even throughout His life on earth He had countless encounters with this evil; from the temptations in the wilderness to His followers desiring to make Him king. Yet, in each encounter Jesus never glanced away from the Father. His obedient and purposeful focus on His heavenly Father never allowed Him to turn His gaze upon Himself, and in Jesus His Son, God Almighty obtained victory over the enemy.

Now we too can have that same victory. Because of the victory of Jesus, when we look to Him instead of ourselves, we overcome self-awareness, put to death the deeds of the flesh and live according to the Spirit. By faith we become dead to ourselves and alive to Christ. But to have the victory, we must know the enemy and know ourselves. If we continue along, fighting someone who is not our enemy, we can never win the war. We have for far too long been fighting with the devil, unaware that he was sent to us by the same God we are praying to for help. He will leave when his assignment is done. It will be done when we see and see rightly. We must come to the place like Job where we recognize that we are the enemy. The enemy is within. Its image is that of me. I am the beast, the one with blasphemous names on my head and with arrogant words and blasphemies coming from my mouth (Revelation 13:1, 5). It is I who am revealed as the man of lawlessness, the son of destruction who opposes and exalts himself above every so-called god or object of worship, so that I take my seat in the temple of God, displaying myself as being God, not unlike one long, long ago (2 Thessalonians 2:3-4) (1 Corinthians 16:9) (Acts 17:24).

Chapter 5

Am I a Christian?

Then and Now

Not long ago I was standing in line at a store and I overheard a conversation behind me. I do not recall anything about the conversation other than hearing one of the participants ask the other if he was a *"Christian."* It is not an uncommon question to hear, but not one I think about often. So, I wondered what my answer would be to such a question. I knew my answer would have as much to do with what being a *Christian* meant to the person who is asking me the question, as it does with who and what I am in relationship to God and man.

To be labeled a Christian was originally a negative inference. It placed you at odds with the world around you. It subjected you to ridicule and harassment at a minimum, but more likely imprisonment and even death. It meant that your leader was a criminal executed for His blasphemy and arrogant trust in God. To be a Christian in the beginning meant you turned your back on your religious heritage. It meant that you no longer considered earth your home. You instantly became an alien in a foreign land and an outcast in your own house. To be called a Christian was to be found guilty of resembling Jesus and His earthly walk of obedience to the Father. To be a Christian meant that apart from Christ you had no life and no purpose, but with Him you had Christ Himself abiding within you.

To be called a *Christian* today does not mean the same thing. Not long after the label "Christian" was coined, its meaning changed. Lost was the divine origin, the eternal life aspect, the lordship of God, the name sake; Christ. The label *Christian* faded in the shadow of religious systems and doctrines. Man sought out to and did use Christianity as a means to meet its own ends. Now, hundreds of years later, modern day Christianity has no resemblance to its origins.

In name, the sons of Israel were the people of God, through whom the glory of the Lord would be made known to the nations. But in practice, Israel was an enemy of God, rebellious and earthly minded. They rejected God as their God and took for themselves false gods to serve their desires. The consequences of their actions are amply recorded in the Bible.

Since the birth of the Church, Christianity has done the same. Other than in name, Christianity has no likeness to Christ. It has rejected the way of the Lord for the way of the world; the way of self. It has turned from a God life back to a Godless life. It has created for itself a god that has the values that it holds dear and that serve its purposes. It has created a god who is called God, but who is not God. It has created a god after the likeness of itself, a god of the flesh and a god of lusts. Less than 40 years after Pentecost, the Apostle Paul wrote to the saints in Philippi about such a people saying, "*They are enemies of the cross of Christ, whose end is destruction, whose god is their appetite, and whose glory is in their shame, who set their minds on earthly things*" (Philippians 3:18-19) (see also, Jude).

If Christians are ridiculed or harassed now, it is because of the gross hypocrisy, not the inherent holiness. To be called a Christian today does not require that there be any likeness to Christ. It is simply a name, but a name without meaning.

There was a time in my life, seventeen years to be exact, when I was very proud to proclaim my Christianity. I embraced the *Christian* faith with everything I had. I walked completely away from a non-Christian life, never looking back. I left an upbringing of Catholicism. I left friends and family. I lived my life as a *Christian* in a "non-Christian" world. I changed the way I spoke. I changed the music I listened to, the shows I watched and the places I went. I did not do things *Christians* were not supposed to do, and I did the things they were supposed to do. At any point during those seventeen years, I would have easily answered yes to the hypothetical question.

After pondering the question for a brief moment and understanding what being a Christian was and should be versus what it has become and is, and assuming that the question was asked with current day Christianity in mind, I concluded my answer now would be, no, I am not a *Christian*.

Changing Sides

It was one Saturday in 2004, while in my blessed *Christian* life, that the Lord revealed Himself to me. That morning I woke up and went to the family room to spend some time with the Lord before the rest of the family awoke. It was a beautiful morning. The sky was a deep blue and the sun was shining brightly. The trees were green, the flowers blooming and my dog was rolling around on the cool green grass having a great time. I recall telling the Lord how blessed I felt in my life. I thanked Him for my wife and children, for my position at the church, my extended family and friends, for all the things He had blessed me with, and I concluded by telling Him how much I loved Him.

He immediately responded to my words with something I never expected to hear. He said, "*You do not love Me. You do not even know what love is.*" I was shocked to say the least. My eyes began to tear. I knew I heard the Lord speak, but I was sure I heard Him wrong. He cannot be speaking to me. Maybe He had the wrong guy. I immediately recalled that I had for years done everything I believed God was asking of me, at least as I was taught it and understood it through Christianity. I prayed regularly. I went to church at every opportunity. I was thankful. I gave joyfully. I served willingly. I worked for the Lord and I left a world behind. So, I repeated in my defense, "But Lord, I *do* love You."

But the Lord did not see it as I saw it. He then responded with an even more staggering word. In my tears, the Lord began to reveal to me that the love that I had for Him was a selfish love, an ungodly love. It was really no love for Him at all, but a love for me. He said most of those who proclaim a faith in Him, who identify themselves as Christians, love Him the same as I did.

He said, "*The love that I have for man consists of the principal part of Me, nothing held back, everything placed on the altar, but the love man has for Me is a peripheral love, and that includes the love that you have for Me.*" The love I had for Him did not include the principal part of me. Regardless of how it was adorned in religious life, it was not real and it was not touching Him.

He likened my love for Him to one who plays a card game in a casino. He explained it's like me walking into a casino and being handed a stack of house chips and invited to play at the blackjack table. I would take the $100 in chips I received and play for an hour turning it into $3,000. But then, the tide would turn and the winning would stop. My chips quickly dwindle to $500, $100, and then $0. At that point I get up from the table and leave. I would play all day with the free chips, but when the free chips were gone I was not willing to invest any of my money in the game. I was not about to reach into my pockets. The Lord then said, "*Such is your love for Me. You have not invested any of yourself in loving Me. Until you do, you cannot know My love.*" As much as I could not believe what He was saying, I knew He was speaking the truth.

I understood for the first time, that the Lord was requiring a death; my death. This was so contrary to my *Christian* faith. This is not what I had embraced all those years before. I believed that He died *FOR* me. I believed that He died to give me life and life more abundantly. And I lived in the faith of all that I had available to me through Christ Jesus, my Lord. But how could I be so off, so wrong. I was suddenly awakened to the reality that I was proclaiming to know God, and I did not, and I believed that He knew me, and He did not.

I took notice of my life. It was as He spoke. So what did the last seventeen years of being a *Christian* amount to if this is where it led me? Well, very little I will say. As I came to see this "Christianity" as He saw it, I wept and repented. Somewhere along the way, I accepted that I was a part of His Church because of a "decision" I made to accept Him as my savior. I lived a prescribed *Christian* life. But none of that counted. As far as God was concerned, I was never born.

It was not until this encounter with the Lord's mercy that I understood the vast distance between the Lord and me. It was not until this time in my life that I could consider the question of whether or not I was a Christian and in my self-analysis, make a judgment based upon Truth instead of belief. It was not until this moment that I could, with great conviction, say that I am not a *Christian*, as that label is understood in today's world.

I understood that morning that being in right-standing with God meant more than what being a Christian meant. I made a decision that day, and have not varied from it, that I would know the Lord and follow Him. It has been a painful, yet wonderful experience, much of which I have written about in other chapters, including, *Faith Perfected, The War of the Lord, and To Know the Lord is to Know His Ways.*

When the Rooster Crowed

Peter experienced some amazing things. He walked on water (Matthew 14:29). He saw the Lord transfigured on the mountaintop (Luke 9:28-36). To him was revealed the true identity of Jesus (Matthew 16:16-17). Not to mention his being called to be a disciple after catching boat loads of fish and all of the shared experiences he had with the other disciples.

Yet, despite this "Christian" life, (I realize Peter was not called a Christian during the days of Jesus' earthly ministry, but I call it his "Christian" life because any Christian today would gladly claim all of Peter's experiences as their own in proclaiming their own "Christianity") Peter was led to the place where he saw that to belong to the Lord; to be a true Christian, it would require more than a belief. It would require a death – his.

All that Peter thought he was and all that he proclaimed to the other disciples and I am sure to the general masses was brought to zero on the night of Jesus' trial, when a young girl called him out for being a *Christian*. Being a *Christian* for the three previous years did not seem so bad to Peter. I mean he "left all to follow" but he still had some pretty nice perks. He healed the sick and raised the dead. Cast out demons and fed the multitudes. But none of that counted until the true meaning of Christianity came upon him when that servant girl came to him and said, *"You too were with Jesus the Galilean."* To which he responded with a resounding denial (Matthew 26:69). The Lord forewarned Peter of this moment when Peter proclaimed his great and unfailing love for Him (Matthew 26:33-35). The rooster crowed and Peter understood.

What Being a Christian Really Means

In the Gospel of Matthew, a company of people, those who called themselves followers of Christ, are told by the Lord at the entrance into the kingdom of heaven to depart for He never knew them (Matthew 7:23). This welcome by Jesus was astonishing to this company because during their lives they prophesied in His name, cast out demons in His name, and in His name performed many miracles (Matthew 7:22).

The words from Jesus, *"Depart from Me...."* are not a parable or a teaching, but a preview of what will actually happen on that day when many will profess His name expecting entrance into the kingdom. Jesus' words should be very disconcerting to anyone who professes His name and should be cause for much concern and personal examination. The Lord's words speak of a people who have a name signifying that they have life, but are dead.

As I stated previously, the Lord made me to understand that for me to have a love that was real, it would require me giving myself to Him. Jesus says to all, *"If anyone wishes to come after Me, he must deny himself, and take up his cross and follow Me"* (Luke 9:23). If we take up our cross and follow Him it will lead us to the place where it led Him; death, then resurrection.

While visiting Israel, I had an opportunity to visit and pray at the Garden of Gethsemane. As I sat there in the garden, looking across the Kidron Valley toward the Antonia Fortress where Jesus was condemned and scourged, the Holy Spirit spoke the most amazing thing. He said, *"Before Jesus took up His cross, before He died on the cross, He died here in the garden."* The Holy Spirit brought to my remembrance Matthew 26:39 when Jesus, while in the garden prays, *"My Father, if it is possible, let this cup pass from Me; yet not as I will, but as You will."*

The Lord said to me, *"Man focuses on the death at the cross **without** understanding the death that first **must** take place in the garden."* Jesus' own words as recorded in Luke 9:23 demonstrate this priority. We must deny ourselves and [then] take up our crosses. As Golgotha represents the place of the crucifixion of the body, Gethsemane represents the place of the death of the will.

If I am going to proclaim my love for the Lord and for that love to be real and accepted by Him, it must include my death. Christianity at its inception looked like death. From every perspective it meant the death of something. Peter learned that lesson. I have learned that lesson. And others have as well. Nevertheless, today, Christianity does not require a death. Is that what your Christianity means to you? Are you like I was, believing that Christ died for me so that I would not have to?

You proclaim your love and allegiance to the Lord. Have you put to death your will, as it was necessary for Christ to do; as it was necessary for the early church to do? If you are carrying your cross (Your Christianity) without having first put to death your will, you are carrying your cross (living out your Christianity) in your own strength, in your own understanding, in your own purpose, and the will of the Father is not being done, as it was allowed to be done by Jesus. If you are carrying your cross in this way, as I was carrying mine, lay it down (repent). Go back to Gethsemane and die there. Then pick up your cross again and allow the Holy Spirit and His grace to lead you down the path to resurrection life; to being a Christian as it was originally meant to be.

✟

Chapter 6

The Answer Is *Not* What You Think

Cultural Disillusionment

Disillusionment is defined as:

That feeling of disappointment resulting from the discovery that something is not as good as one believed it to be.[1]

In almost every case, the source of the disillusionment lies not with the object of the disillusion, but with the bearer of the belief. The disillusionment is usually the result of unfounded confidence or ignorance of the truth. If the truth was known or the confidence found to be misplaced, disillusionment would not occur. Disillusionment can appear in any area of human life, and as long as one remains blind to the truth, the disillusionment can lead to anger, offense, alienation or worse. Spiritual disillusionment is simply man's disillusionment as it relates to God.

Some disillusionment is the result of innocence. However, most is the result of stubbornness. The former usually passes away with time. The latter grows progressively worse as time goes by. The progression of the latter is fostered by our burying the truth under a sea of ideological tradition. We romanticize our ideals and beliefs, making the truth out to be that which we want to believe.

Regardless of the culture in which we live, we all want to believe in a world where you make your gift list, give it to Santa Claus and he delivers. On Christmas Day you would arise to open every requested present. It would be the perfect day. The reality is that at some point, you asked for that most wonderful gift that only Santa could deliver, as he has so often in the past, but this time he did not. First, sadness sets in because you did not get what you wanted. But then something deeper happens. You question the existence of Santa, the existence of the North Pole. Which leads one to wonder just what else has mom and dad lied to you about? Oh, the devastation to everything in the world you knew!

We recognize that our ideological traditions produce disappointment, nevertheless, the hope that we place in them makes us feel better, so we perpetuate them. We would rather think upon our happy ideals than face reality.

I would venture to say that we have all experienced this type of disappointment at some level, probably not with Santa, but maybe with a valued relationship, possessing the "American Dream" or some other romanticized ideal. We want to believe in that kind of world so much we are willing to deny reality and continue to live as though it exists, and in the case of Santa, even going so far as to fill our children's hearts with these ideological traditions which will ultimately lead to *their* future disappointment. Ridiculously childish argument you say? I say not. It is simply the shadow of a greater evil.

Spiritual Disillusionment

The greater evil is that our ideological tradition extends to God Himself. We want with all our heart to believe that God cares about our every concern. We have been taught and we continue to teach that if it concerns me, it concerns God. We just need to ask Him for whatever we want, in His name of course, and we are confident its arrival is eminent. We have deceived ourselves to the extent that we even consider the written Word to be the prescribed gift list; the spiritual Sears' catalog. Just order it and it is yours.

We have so idealized and romanticized God that the God of our ideological tradition is nothing more than the divine Santa Claus, there to respond to our needs and our wants. If nothing else, this falsehood within Christianity has harvested generations of spiritual infancy. But the most common result is spiritual disillusionment that can ultimately lead to death when God does not respond according to our expectations and we become offended and in many cases we simply walk away from Him.

For every situation we encounter there is a response to be made. The response reveals in us either Life or Death. *"For the one who sows to his own flesh will from the flesh reap corruption, but the one who sows to the Spirit will from the Spirit reap eternal life"* (Galatians 6:8). Remember, disillusionment is usually the result of unfounded confidence or ignorance of the truth. If the truth is known or the confidence is found to be misplaced, disillusionment would not occur. The best way to deal with disillusionment is to know the truth. The best way to deal with spiritual disillusionment is to know God.

Much of the spiritual disillusionment found within Christianity is the result of a wrong understanding of Scripture. Most Scripture has been used or taught in such a way as to perpetuate Christian ideological traditions. These teachings are not supported by Scripture, yet most of them are believed to be accurate and true. To illustrate, I will provide here a list of verses taken from the Gospels of Matthew and Luke. Read through the list. Get out your Bible and read the verses.

The statements following the (➢) are what are generally believed to be true, and such beliefs are used to perpetuate ideological traditions. The statements following the (•) are the Truth. See where you fall in your beliefs. See whether or not you are set up to be a victim of spiritual disillusionment because of a wrong understanding of God and who He is and how He operates.

The List

- ➢ It is believed that He is concerned about our current occupation, or its continuation (Matthew 4:19);

    - • Yet, He says to us follow Me, I will make you fishers of men. He does not sound too concerned with our careers.

- ➢ It is believed that He is concerned if we are being persecuted (Matthew 5:11; 44);

    - • Yet, He says rejoice and intercede for those who persecute you. We most often ask Him to end the persecution.

- ➢ It is believed that He is concerned if we are insulted (Matthew 5:11);

    - • Yet, He says rejoice, they did the same to Me. I have heard Christians ask God to kill the one who has insulted them.

- ➢ It is believed that He is concerned if someone speaks falsely and evil against my faith (Matthew 5:11);

    - • Yet, He says rejoice, you are Mine.

- ➢ It is believed that He is concerned if we have been wronged (Matthew 5:25);

    - • Yet, He says forgive, that you may be forgiven. Forgiveness given to others is probably the single most neglected act of worship.

- ➤ It is believed that He is concerned if we are being sued or required to go an extra mile (Matthew 5:42);

  - Yet, we are instructed to give to who asks of us and do not turn away from him who wants to borrow. We usually resist here because we are concerned how this will affect us if we relent.

- ➤ It is believed that He is concerned if we are hated, even if it is for His name's sake (Matthew 5:44);

  - Yet, we are commanded to love in return.

- ➤ It is believed that He is concerned if we lack of food or clothing (Matthew 6:33);

  - Yet, He says seek His kingdom and righteousness, and He will provide all.

- ➤ It is believed that He is concerned about our future (Matthew 6:34);

  - Yet, He says live for today, tomorrow will care for itself.

- ➤ It is believed that He is impressed if we prophesy, cast out demons, or perform miracles (Matthew 7:22-23);

  - When He says, only seek to be known by Him.

- ➤ It is believed that He is concerned when a flood comes upon us (Matthew 7:24-27);

  - Yet, He advises to build upon the Rock and don't worry about the flood.

- ➤ It is believed that He is concerned when a loved one has died and needs burial (Matthew 8:22);

- Yet, He stated let the dead bury the dead, you follow Me.

➢ It is believed that He cares if we are in a life threatening situation (Matthew 8:26);

- Yet, He commands me to not be afraid. Have faith.

➢ It is believed that He is concerned if those I preach to do not heed my words. (Matthew 10:14);

- Yet, His orders were, move on! Wipe off the dust.

➢ It is believed that He cares if we are brought before the courts because of Him. (Matthew 10:17);

- Yet, He said beforehand not to be afraid. The Holy Spirit will speak through you.

➢ It is believed that He cares if we are betrayed unto death by parent or child (Matthew 10:21-22);

- Yet, He urges me to endure to the end.

➢ It is believed that He would be concerned if we were to experience death in my flesh at the hands of men (Matthew 10:28);

- Yet, He warns, fear Him who is able to destroy both body and soul in hell.

➢ It is believed that He cares that we are weary or heavy-laden (Matthew 11:28-30);

- Yet, He invites us to come to Him and find rest for our souls.

- It is believed that He cares about our seemingly insurmountable circumstances (Matthew 14:17);

  - Yet, He commands us to give them something to eat.

- It is believed that He is concerned about our wealth (or the maintaining or keeping of it) (Matthew 19:21);

  - When He says to sell my possessions, and give to the poor and come and follow Me.

- It is believed that He cares if I have been serving Him longer than those around me (Matthew 20:14);

  - He responds to my grumbling by reminding me that we agreed to a wage. "Take what is yours and go."

- It is believed that He cares who is in political or economic power (Matthew 22:21);

  - When He answered by saying, "Give to Caesar what is Caesar's."

- It is believed that He cares if we are in jail for our faith and doubting His word (Luke 7:23);

  - Yet, He says blessed is he who does not take offense at Me.

- It is believed that He cares if there is division within my house (Luke 12:53);

  - Yet, He prophesied that father would be against son and mother against daughter, etc.

> It is believed that He cares that we keep the Law (Luke 13:10-17; 14:1-6; 18:21);

- Yet, He healed on the Sabbath and keeping all the law did not count much for the rich young ruler.

> It is believed that He is impressed if we must leave our home and family to follow Him (Luke 18:28);

- Yet, He says who will not receive many times as much in the age to come?

> It is believed that He does care when all appears lost and our hope is gone (Luke 24:19-26);

- Yet, He responds with, "O foolish man, slow to believe what has been spoken."

> It is believed that He does care that I have bought a piece of land, purchased five yoke of oxen, or married a wife (Luke 14:20);

- Yet, He warns that if I refuse His invitation, I will not eat at His banquet.

So, how many of these have been found on your prayer lists? How many tears have been shed pleading for His intervention in the things concerning us? How many times have we awakened with such eager expectation, only to stare reality square in the face? Entire Christian ministries and church services have been dedicated to a god of our making. We have believed that our God is a good God, meaning, He will be good to ME, as we have defined good. This has led to many broken hearts.

The problem is that we love God and believe He loves us when and only when everything in our life is taken care of; when our pressing concerns are handled by Him. And when He does not seem to be handling anything that concerns us, we question His love, His presence, even His existence.

Let me ask a question. Did God not love or was He not concerned for Jacob's youngest son, Joseph? If you evaluate Joseph's life by the ideological tradition under which most, if not all Christians currently live, he was neither loved nor concerned for. First, God set him up for failure by giving him a dream that would make him an outcast in his father's house. Second, God allowed him to be betrayed, sold into slavery, imprisoned, and threatened with death. If and when this happens today, Christians usually respond in one of two ways. They either start rebuking Satan or they get offended at God's apparent lack of concern for their plight. Their rebuking only reveals their blindness to the purpose and ways of the Lord (see *The War of the Lord*). Their offense reveals their love of self (see *To Know the Lord, is to Know His Ways*).

Let us understand this truth: Our God IS a good God, but as He defines the term. God is only concerned with bringing us to Himself; and that by way of His Son, Jesus. He will and has done everything to accomplish THAT purpose as it "concerns" you (Psalm. 138:8). He purposes that in all things, Christ is your answer.

So, if you were to ask me if God is concerned with your [fill-in the blank], I would answer, no, He is not. Probably, not the answer you expected. But I would also say to you that He is concerned that you would know and trust Him and your trust in Him would be evidenced by your obedience to His will.

Our freedom from spiritual disillusionment is found in forsaking our ideological tradition of a "concerned" God, and embracing the true God. In Him we have eternal life. Eternal Life is to know Him, the only true God, and Jesus Christ whom He sent (John 17:3). Eternal Life is not being free from hardship, but persevering in hardship through the One who has overcome. He says, *"In the world you have tribulation, but take courage, I have overcome the world"* (John 16:33). Belief in that will leave no one disappointed.

Why don't we today destroy this ideological tradition and embrace the Truth and be set free? God is not in the Christmas gift business. He is not in the business of giving you the life that you love. He is, however, about giving you a life that loves you; a life eternal; a life with Him. That Life is obtained, not by having the Christian version of all that the world has to offer or by having everything in your life go just the way you want, but by dying to your own life and its desires and lusts, so that the Life of Christ may reign in you (see Luke 14:26-27, 33; 16:19-31; Mark 10:17-22).

So how about we stop asking for God to bless us, and let us for once bless Him? Well, how do we do that? We do that by believing in Him, not in a god of our own design. We do that by believing Him. For when we believe Him, we can say that though

> *"we are afflicted in every way, we are not crushed; perplexed, but not despairing; persecuted, but not forsaken; struck down, but not destroyed; always carrying about in the body the dying of Jesus, so that the life of Jesus also may be manifested in our body. For we who live are constantly being delivered over to death for Jesus' sake, so that the life of Jesus also may be manifested in our mortal flesh"* (2 Corinthians 4:8-11).

✦

Chapter 7

WHAT GOD THINKS

The Words of Life

Read: Isaiah 55:2b-3a; Proverbs 4; and Matthew 4:4.

The verse that gives the most direct light to what the Lord wants to show us at this time is found in Isaiah 55:3, which states,

> *"Give ear and come to Me;*
> *Listen, that you may live."*

The Lord God says so much. He says much more than we hear. We seldom hear Him because we are not in the position of listening. We are usually too preoccupied with our circumstances or *our* will to even give attention to His voice. But when we position (humble) ourselves to hear His voice, Oh, He says so much (John 8:47)! He will instruct you as to when and what to speak. He will instruct you as to when and where to travel. He may instruct you to help someone or to continue on past a person. He may have you buy one thing or sell another. He may say, "Arise!" or He may say, "Rest!" There is no limit to what He may say to you and what He says to you is necessary, vital, and always for your good. But as verse three above shows, there is something more to the words He speaks. There is a place in the Lord, well past just hearing His words that He desires His disciples to reach. It is the place where the disciple understands what He *thinks* about the things He speaks. What He says to you and what He thinks about what He says to you are not the same. To the Lord, the words that He speaks are life to all of creation. Jesus communicated this truth to us when He said, "MAN SHALL NOT LIVE ON BREAD ALONE, BUT ON EVERY WORD THAT PROCEEDS OUT OF THE MOUTH OF GOD" (Matthew 4:4).

As I stated, He will instruct you what to speak or what to do at a particular time. The instruction He there provides should be obeyed exactly. Nevertheless, the details of what He has you to speak or to do are vastly different from why He wants you to speak or to do them. The Lord wants us to gain understanding as to the difference. When we acquire such an understanding, we will know Him better and we will hear Him more.

This truth about the Lord and His words was communicated to man from the beginning. The Lord God said to Adam,

"From any tree of the garden you may eat freely; but from the tree of the knowledge of good and evil you shall not eat, for in the day that you eat from it you will surely die" (Genesis 2:16-17).

Contained within these two verses is the entirety of God's heart concerning His words. The first thing we find in this passage is the specific instruction "*... you shall not eat*" which Adam is to follow. The instruction, whether understood or not, is for his good and is to be obeyed. The next thing found in this passage, and the thing with which we are presently concerned is what God thought about what He instructed Adam. His thought concerning His words to Adam is summed up in the last phrase of verse 17 where He says, "*For in the day that you eat from it you will surely die.*" If I may paraphrase that statement to explain what the Lord is showing it would read, "Adam, My words, all of them, are life to you. The day that you do not live by My words, you shall surely die."

How easy it is for man to disregard the words of the Lord as having little or no value. He treats them most of the time as if they were never spoken. Man always thinks he knows best. The human mind finds such assurance in itself, never realizing the necessity of trusting in the Sovereign Almighty. It is not until the heart overtakes the mind that man can step away from himself and move towards the Lord.

When you arrive at the place where you know not only what God said, but also what He thinks about what He said, you see that the sin that separated Adam from fellowship with God was not so much the act of eating of the forbidden tree, as it was not understanding that he lived by every word of God. His fellowship was broken because he failed to trust God's words to him. If he had understanding as to that and that alone, he would have valued the Lord's words more highly than he did and he would not have departed from His instruction. The act was not the sin. What caused the act was the sin.

What was recovered by Jesus was the value of God's word. A man once again considered God's words to be words of life. We mistakenly think that there was something special or unique about the person of Jesus that brought Him to speak only as the Father spoke and to do only as the Father did (John 12:49-50). The only uniqueness was in the superlative value that Jesus placed upon the words of His Father. Jesus was not able to do this because He came from Heaven. He was able to do this because He completely surrendered to God, trusting and obeying Him in everything. (see Philippian 2:7-8). The truth is that this is a necessity for all men. It is what Adam failed to do and it is what Jesus did perfectly. If you do as Jesus did and live by every word that proceeds forth from the mouth of the Father you will reap life. If you do as Adam did, not heeding the words of the Father or acting as you have seen Him act, you will reap death. In either case, what must be appreciated is that the words of the Lord are preeminent and life is only found in finding and heeding them.

The Father's Instruction

We gain further insight into the heart of the Lord concerning His words from Proverbs Four. There the Lord declares,

> "*Hear, O sons ... and give attention that you may gain understanding; ...Let your heart hold fast My words, keep my commandments and live*" (Proverbs 4:1, 4).

Again this is what God thinks about the things He says, the things that come out of His mouth to your ears and to your heart. In other words, the Lord says something to you; His thought about whatever, and about that thing He says, "Keep what I have said to you; obey My words and you will live."

The entirety of the fourth Proverb reveals this fundamental message. This Proverb speaks of "wisdom" which is referred to by the use of the feminine personal pronouns "her" and "she" as in verse six where Solomon writes, "*Do not forsake her, and she will guard you, love her and she will watch over you.*" In these statements the Lord is metaphorically speaking of the words that proceed forth from His mouth. Of those words, He says, "love them and do not forsake them. These words will guard you and watch over you."

In the preceding verse five He says, "*Acquire [the words from My mouth]... Do not forget or turn away from [them].*" Again, in verse seven He says, "*The beginning of wisdom is: Acquire wisdom; and with all your acquiring, get understanding.*" In other words, the beginning of wisdom is to hear from God; to acquire it. The beginning of wisdom is to get wisdom, and wisdom comes from His mouth. The next verse continues with, *"Prize her, and she will exalt you; She will honor you if you embrace her."* Do not get lost in the Lord's use of these feminine personal pronouns. In each instance He is speaking of His words. I should prize the word that comes forth from His mouth to me and that word will exalt me. It will honor me if I embrace it. According to verse nine, it will place on my head a garland of grace. What is a garland of grace? It is the power of God. The word of God is power unto me as I obey Him, and His word will present me with a crown of beauty.

In verse ten we see again the Father's declaration first seen in verse one. It is clear from both verses that the Lord is referring to His words and His admonition each time is, "Hear them." Notice also the fruit of hearing and accepting His words; it is life (see also Proverbs 4:13, 20, 22-23).

Verses eleven and twelve reveal to us the activity of God towards His disciples as it relates to His words. He declares,

"I have directed you in the way of wisdom; I have led you in upright paths. When you walk, your steps will not be impeded; and if you run, you will not stumble."

What does that mean? It means He is directing us to the place where we are hearing His voice. In most Christian circles these verses have been understood to mean that God is directing our earthly path; our temporal walk, so that we do not walk down a dark path; so that our way in this world is made clear. Christianity has taught and believes that because of a profession of faith the Lord is with us wherever we go. So much of the Christian life is done with this assurance of the "nearness" of God. However, that is not what the Lord is speaking by this passage. That is not "the way of wisdom." First of all, the Lord is not with us wherever we go. If we are not FOLLOWING Him, He is not with us. He does not follow after man. Man must follow after God.

What is the way of wisdom? Hearing His voice is the way of wisdom. Let's back up a little. The beginning of wisdom is to acquire wisdom. The way of wisdom comes from the Lord. What comes from the Lord is His word. He draws and directs man to seek and live by His word.

The true meaning of these verses is, as I walk to Him I will not be impeded. When I seek to hear His voice I will not be stopped. My way to the Lord will never be forbidden. In these verses the Lord is describing the pathway to Him, not the pathway through our earthly existence. Most Christians count themselves blessed and give glory to God when earthly obstacles are removed from before them. However, few ever see the impediments blocking their way to God. The greatest blessing to man is unhindered access to the Father. This blessing of "the way of wisdom" is magnified in light of the Lord's word recorded in Isaiah 55:6:

"Seek Me while I may be found."

The Way of Evil Men

"The way of the wicked is like darkness" (Proverbs 4:19). It is the opposite of the way of wisdom (see 4:18). In verses 14 and 15, the Lord admonishes us *"not [to] enter the path of the wicked and not [to] proceed in the way of evil men. Avoid it, do not pass by it; turn away from it and pass on."* The way of evil men is to do their own will and not seek the will of the Lord. It is the nature of man. It is what Israel did continually (see Judges 2:11-12; 3:5-8, 12-14; 4:1-3; 6:1-2; 10:6-8; 13:1). They forsook the Lord. They repeatedly disregarded the words of His mouth. They did not regard His words as life, hence they failed to seek His will or even desire to hear from Him. They simply proceeded in their own will and wisdom (see Jeremiah. 17:13).

We are all susceptible to entering the path of the wicked. Even men like Joshua, David, and Solomon proceeded in the way of evil men: Joshua at Ai; David in numbering his men and moving the Ark of the Covenant; and Solomon in building altars to other gods. The way of evil men is to go away from God. God speaks something to you and you turn away from what He said and you go about your business. That is the path of the wicked. Rejecting what He said. When you reject what He says you are rejecting Him. Cursed is the man who rejects the Lord (Jeremiah 17:5-6).

You must treat disregarding the word of the Lord as if such indifference were leprosy. Think about how hard this is when the Lord speaks to you something and all the reasoned voices around you are saying disregard it. You start consulting with other people about what you heard. That is the worst thing you can do. Trusting in man is wrong and can lead you away from God. Man is naturally inclined to do his own will, not the will of the Father. Man, not surrendered to God,

> *"Cannot sleep unless [he does] evil; unless [he makes] someone stumble. For [he eats] the bread of wickedness and [drinks] the wine of violence"* (Proverbs 4:16-17) (see also Job 32 and 42).

Do you think Jesus, while here on earth, ever asked anyone, even His disciples, what they thought about something that the Father spoke to Him? No, He did not. So why would you? If you say you belong to Christ, you are to walk as He walked (1 John 2:6).

The Bread of Wickedness And the Wine of Violence

What is this bread of wickedness? What is this wine of violence? It is refusing to walk in the way of wisdom. It is failing to hear and obey the word of the Lord. The violence and wickedness is against the words of God.

You probably think Cain's wickedness was the act of blood violence against his brother Able. That was not the problem. The wickedness and violence were against the Lord because Cain did not listen to the Lord when He told him to turn from his way and Cain refused to listen (see Genesis 4:6-7). That wickedness was worse than the shedding of blood. If Cain would have received the word of the Lord and allowed his heart to be softened and broken, the act of violence would not have taken place. The greater evil was the act against God, not against his brother. Cain rejected the word that the Lord gave him. That was the true violence. Wisdom was rejected. Cain went the other way. Cain went the way of wickedness. If he had gone the way of wisdom, his brother would not have died that day. Do you see where the sin is?

More than likely you would not raise your hand against your sibling, but daily you do the same thing Cain did against God. You would not strike dead your brother or your sister, but you would reject the word of the Lord just as easily as Cain did. Do you see where the violence lies? Do you see the way of evil men?

The Straight and Narrow

"Let your eyes look directly ahead and let your gaze be fixed straight in front of you. Watch the path of your feet and all your ways will be established. Do not turn to the right nor to the left; turn your foot from evil" (Proverbs 4:25-27).

"Turn your foot from evil." This is a very interesting statement because immediately before that the Lord says "do not turn to the right nor to the left." These two statements seem to contradict but they do not. How do you turn your foot from evil, yet neither turn to the right nor to the left? Simple; turning your foot from evil is to not go to the left or to the right, but to continue straight ahead. Fix your eyes directly ahead. Directly ahead of you is the word He has spoken. It is the direction in which wisdom is found. Guard it, for it is your life (4:13).

The supreme treasure in all that we have covered thus far is that, regardless of what the Lord may speak, the fact that *He* spoke it means there is life. The fact that the words came from *His* mouth is value enough. When you understand that then it does not matter what comes out of His mouth, you will hold it dear. The Lord knows you are inclined to be grateful for the things that come out of His mouth that you appreciate or desire. But, He also knows that when you hear something that you do not appreciate, because you are thinking in an earthly way, you are more inclined to disregard it. But if you understand what the Lord is revealing to us here, it will not matter what comes out of His mouth. You will treasure it and hold it dear because now you know what He thinks about *everything* that comes out of His mouth. That prepares you to accept everything from Him. It is no longer a matter of what is said, but Who said it.

Jeremiah 17:7-8 says, "*Blessed is the man who trusts in the Lord and whose trust is the Lord. For he will be like a tree planted by the water, that extends its roots by a stream and will not fear when the heat comes, but its leaves will be green, and it will not be anxious in a year of drought nor cease to yield fruit.*" The emphasis here is the second part of verse seven, "*whose trust is the Lord.*"

When your trust is the Lord, He is free to speak anything and everything to you knowing that you will value His words, not for the words themselves, but for the One who spoke them. In other words, it does not matter what comes, because your trust is the Lord, you will live by His every word, whatever that word may be. The distinction is subtle, yet enormous.

When your trust is the Lord, your life will be a fulfillment of the previous verse. Like the tree whose leaves are green and yielding fruit in a year of drought, you will live a life in contradiction to your surrounding environment. There may be heat and drought, yet you are green and yielding fruit. You will be doing what cannot be done. How? It will be so because your trust is the Lord, and in Him is found Life. This is the place in the Lord, where He desires His disciples to reach. Will you go there?

✦

Chapter 8

Satisfied

STOP!!! Do not read past this first paragraph. Get pen and paper or if you are up to speed on today's technology, open the memo app on your phone or tablet. I would ask that you make a few notes before you begin reading this chapter. I would like you to write down what first went through your mind when you read the chapter title. What entered your mind when your eyes ran across the title *Satisfied?* Do *not* go looking for a dictionary or a thesaurus. Other than that, there are no limitations or qualifications on your response. Whatever it meant to you when you first read the title, write that down; make note of it. Did the word first raise questions or elicit a direct response? If so, write it down. If it raised questions, could you or did you answer those questions?

No one except you and God will see your answers to this exercise. It is necessary for you to be honest with yourself if you expect to get anything out of this chapter. Be careful not to think about or for someone else. Focus on yourself and your life. Record your answer to the question before you read further.

———————————

If you have completed the task given on the previous pages, I will now tell you that the Lord presented me with the same undertaking one evening. When I heard Him speak the word "satisfied" I interpreted it as a question and I simply responded, "I am. I am satisfied." The Lord then brought me to two verses of Scripture: Proverbs 27:20 and Matthew 5:6.

In Proverbs 27:20 the Lord states,
"Sheol and Abaddon are never satisfied, nor are the eyes of man ever satisfied."

In Matthew 5:6 Jesus says,
"Blessed are those who hunger and thirst for righteousness, for they shall be satisfied."

The obvious link between these verses is the presence of the word *satisfied*; the former in the context of it never materializing and the latter in the context of it reaching fulfillment.

SATISFIED - The word seems simple enough; pretty straight forward; not too intimidating. But that word SATISFIED has the potential of being THE word that distinguishes the sheep from the goats, the wheat from the tares, and eternal life from eternal death. It has among its synonyms the words *completeness* and *contentment*.[1] So it can be said that if you are satisfied you are therefore complete and content and if you are not satisfied you are therefore not complete nor content.

After leading me to the two verses above, the Lord began to show me how when the heart of man is filled with a desire, any desire, other than a desire for *Him*, He is unable to be that soul's satisfaction. The Lord then said to me,

> *"I am the One who satisfies and I can only satisfy the one who* **can** *be satisfied."*

Despite my proclamation to Him that I was satisfied, here was an opportunity for further self-examination. I understood that the Lord was placing before me the challenge: *"if you are led by the desires of your heart you can never be satisfied. Hell will be satisfied before you will and hell is never going to be satisfied"* (Matthew 6:23; 15:19; Mark 7:21; Jeremiah 17:9).

I immediately thought about my day. What was on my mind when I woke up? What about when I saw my children before they went off to school, or the conversations with my wife during the day? And what about the several tasks that I needed to complete before the evening? I asked myself if I had been led by the desires of my heart. At that moment I could not identify where I had done so, especially at the expense of obeying the voice of the Lord. I then considered that each day contains such an opportunity for satisfaction. I saw that the only way to be satisfied was to be satisfied in today. When I look beyond today I will not be satisfied because desire abides in my tomorrow (Matthew 6:34). This dissatisfaction with today is a part of the sinful nature of man. It is the evidence of self-awareness and self-will. Each day I must find my satisfaction in God alone. I must turn my heart's eye toward the right now and be content, complete, and satisfied in where He has brought me and have no desire for any other thing. It became clearer that as a husband, father, son, brother, friend, and even as a fellow man, the Lord continually gives me opportunities to find satisfaction in Him and where He leads me. I purposed to exercise my freewill to continue to find my satisfaction in God at each opportunity.

I then began to see that it only takes one thought to lead me so far away because it is that thought that gives birth to a desire that burns in my heart that God cannot satisfy with Himself. It is not that God cannot or will not give to me what is the desire of my heart. It is only that the Person of God will not be the fulfillment of that desire unless He and He alone is the object of my desire.

The Lord then had me reflect on the heart desire of the sons of Israel, as when they asked to go spy out the land that He had commanded that they go and take without fear. The Lord gave to them what they asked for (their heart desire), to spy out the land, which resulted in their eventual demise in the wilderness because after spying out the land they became fearful and rebelled against the Lord's command (Deuteronomy 1:19-33; Numbers 14:26-35). I also considered this same people, a few generations removed, desiring to be ruled by an earthly king like the other peoples of the earth. Again, the Lord gave to them their desire, but again it was not Him in whom they found satisfaction (1 Samuel 8:4-7; Hosea 13: 9-11).

I also saw where Adam and Eve let their desires lead them to dissatisfaction which led to sin which brought about death (Genesis 3:6, 21). And desire for something or someone other than God Himself led Cain to fill his appetite with the blood of his brother (Genesis 4:3-8), and the sons of Israel to feed their desire with the wealth of Jericho instead of the word of the Lord (Joshua 7:11), and the sons of Jacob to feed their desire with the life of their brother, Joseph. None of these found satisfaction in God Himself, in what He spoke to them, or in where He had led them. Instead they sought out their heart's desire (that thing that they wanted more than God Himself or His word) and obtained it, and yet remained unsatisfied.

As I considered all that the Lord was showing me, I began to understand that He satisfies the one who hungers and thirsts after a relationship of right standing with Him (Psalm 37:4). He cannot satisfy *with Himself* the one who does not have that hunger or that thirst. I also saw that the man who finds himself in right relationship with the Lord is satisfied not only in his relationship with God but in all that God brings him (Philippians 2:8).

Take the Apostle Paul for example, who said that he "*learned to be content in whatever circumstances*" he found himself because his strength was Christ (Philippians 4:11-13). On several occasions Paul found himself in a comfortable place among brethren eager to hear the truth, only to find himself a few hours later chained to a prison wall with no food, no water, no shoes, and no friends. That happened to him at least five times. Yet, in all that, Paul was satisfied in God and satisfied in whatever God presented to him.

When I do not find my satisfaction in God and instead let my heart's desire lead me forward I become confused and in my confusion I am led into further error and sin.

Such was the case for David when he did not find satisfaction in God or in His word (2 Samuel 11, 12). So too with his son Solomon whose desire led him to taste every pleasure under the sun only to find himself building altars to other gods to satisfy the desire of his many wives (Ecclesiastes 2:1; 1 Kings 11:1-13). Consider also the confusion of John the Baptist. His calling was completed at the revelation of the Messiah, for he was His forerunner (John 1:31, 35-37; 3:28). Yet, it was desire that led him to continue in that which by his own words was to decrease (John 3:30). His desire ushered in confusion that ultimately led him to question the identity of the very One he proclaimed (Matthew 11:3; John 1:36).

The Word says that *those who hunger and thirst for righteousness shall be satisfied.* Hungering and thirsting after righteousness requires an obedient act on the part of the hearer. In our three examples the obedience was lacking. (2 Samuel 12:9; 1 Kings 11:9-10; Luke 7:22-23). In such instances, unless there is repentance from the dissatisfaction (2 Samuel 12:13-14), the confusion will ultimately lead to death, and for some it did. For more on this topic, read *Confusion.*

Occasionally the required obedience is not so clear cut. There are times when hungering and thirsting for righteousness requires an obedience of rest. Sometimes the Lord does not speak, or if He does, He speaks only a little or says something other than what you want to hear. If the Lord is silent or if the Lord has given only partial revelation, be content in and with the word that the Lord has spoken or that He has yet to speak. Do not seek more than He has given at the moment; rest. Otherwise, you are demonstrating your dissatisfaction with Him or what He has given. In those times, God has given you a measure of Himself and if you have not found that to be satisfying you are demonstrating your selfishness (Exodus 16:4).

On many occasions the Lord has tested my satisfaction with Him in this way. Whether or not it is a part of your belief in God, you must understand that He will test our trustworthiness and our faithfulness to Him by His silence. It is in those times when He is not speaking that I understand His desire for me to find satisfaction in Him, as opposed to what He speaks. When God is silent, I rest confidently in His silence, staying alert as to my impatience as a sign of unbelief and selfish desire. (For more on this read *What God Thinks*).

One reason we find it so hard to rest in God is that we have deceived ourselves into believing that our beating down God's door is a sign of our spiritual hunger. We endlessly petition God to change our circumstances. We cry out for "more of Him" (John 6:26). However, this dissatisfaction with our life or our situation disguised in prayer and interpreted as passion for Him, is nothing other than the manifestation of self-will and self-awareness. It should not be understood as spiritual hunger or satisfaction in God.

An example of this is seen in the life of Hannah. She was one of the two wives of Elkanah. The other wife, Peninnah had children and Hannah did not. Year after year Peninnah would provoke Hannah because of her barrenness. One year, while sacrificing to the Lord at the temple in Shiloh, Hannah wept bitterly before the Lord, vowing to Him that if she were given a son that she would give her son to the Lord all of the days of his life (1 Samuel 1:1-11). She received a son whose name was Samuel, who became a judge and prophet of Israel (1 Samuel 1:20; 3:20). It is mistakenly believed that this was a righteous act by Hannah. It was anything but. The entire episode was a manifestation of her self-awareness (her pain from the provocation of Peninnah), born out of her desire for something more (justification and revenge), that grew from her dissatisfaction with God and where He had brought her. It would not have happened as it did if she would have only been satisfied with Him.

At the outset God asked her, through the words of Elkanah, "*Why is your heart sad? Am I not better to you than ten sons*?" In the face of her torment and her desire to change her circumstances, the answer was a resounding NO! She wanted a son and needed a son to quash her rival and what her rival was doing to her and she was willing to sacrifice her own child to accomplish it. It did not matter to Hannah that the Lord, through her husband, expressed that His great love for her was not dependent upon her giving him sons (1 Samuel 1:5).

So now that you have made it to the end of the chapter, revisit your answers from the beginning of the chapter. What entered your mind when your eyes ran across the title *Satisfied?* Did you think it to be a question or a statement? Did you answer yes, I am satisfied or no, I am not satisfied? Or did you respond by asking what does satisfied mean? Your honesty with yourself will determine how far you go with the Lord in this matter.

If you could not answer because you were not sure what satisfied meant, then that is a very strong indication that you have yet to experience satisfaction. When you are satisfied you know it. If you answered, yes, I am satisfied, then is it a satisfaction in the Lord Himself? When you first thought about the word, did your thoughts lead you to conclude that regardless what the day looks like, good, bad, or indifferent I am satisfied with it; I am complete in it; and I am content in it because He is enough, so I am satisfied (Psalm 118:24)? Or did your yes answer lead you to dwell upon a recently fulfilled desire? And finally, if you answered no, I am not satisfied, can you now identify why you are not satisfied? Are you asking Him for something; something like a king, or a son, or an opportunity to spy out the land or anything of the sort? Be careful what you ask. You will get it, but it is not what He wants for you.

The conclusion to be drawn from this chapter is that those who are satisfied in God will spend eternity with Him, entering into His rest and experiencing His satisfaction in them. On the other hand, those who never find a satisfaction in God during their time here on earth will spend eternity apart from Him, experiencing His dissatisfaction in them (Matthew 25:31-46).

He wants to satisfy you with Himself. If you hunger and thirst after a relationship of right-standing with Him, you will be satisfied. However, if your appetite is your heart's desire and that desire is not Him, you will likely partake in that meal, but your desire will never be appeased. Bon Appétit.

Chapter 9

Confusion

Like death, it is no respecter of persons. Young and old, rich and poor, male and female all experience confusion. It is defined as a state of being perplexed or disconcerted or being disoriented with regard to one's sense of time, place, or identity.[1] Despite its universal effect on man, few people understand its cause or know how to alter its course. Not that there is a shortage of opinion as to what it is or why it occurs, it is just that the opinions, regardless of how scholarly, only prove how little man understands it, thus explaining why mankind still suffers from this unabated malady.

Before we go further into accurately explaining confusion, its cause, its effect, and its cure, I would like to share a true story.

One day a young man became interested in acquiring a guitar. The next day he visited a store specializing in the instrument. He saw some models that interested him but decided that he could find something better elsewhere. That evening he purposed to visit another store that had more of a selection. So he went to bed with plans to shop the next day. He awoke at 4:00 a.m. to get ready for his college classes. As he was dressing for school and thinking about his upcoming day the Lord said to him, "*Do not buy a guitar.*" He understood the sternness of the Lord's words and was very disappointed that the Lord said this to him. His disappointment continued as he held on to his desire for a new guitar.

As he was driving to school he was trying to make sense of what he heard God say and why God may have said it. In his spirit he knew what the Lord said. But in his flesh he felt that buying the guitar was innocent. He then began trying to reason how he could buy a guitar and still be okay with God. By the time he arrived at the school he had grown tired of arguing within and just decided to stop thinking about it and go to class.

Several hours later classes were over and the thoughts of the morning returned to the forefront of his mind. He sat in the parking lot of the school desiring more than ever to drive straight to the store and buy the guitar. He told the Lord, "*Look Lord, I want this guitar, I just want it to be okay with You.*" With those thoughts he proceeded to the store. He decided he would just go and look at the guitars and make a decision after that. As he drove to the store he recognized that he was proceeding alone. He knew that God was not leading him to go to the store, but he continued nonetheless. Within minutes he arrived at his destination. As he approached the door of the store he no longer felt any conflict within. As conflicting as the morning had been, now that he was in the store he seemed to feel more in control of his thoughts and plans. He found himself standing in front of an array of guitars with a host of store personnel ready and willing to assist him. He was no longer questioning whether or not he should be at the store. Now he became conflicted over which color guitar he liked and how much he was willing to pay for it.

Despite what he heard only hours before, it was not long until he found himself at the register with the perfect guitar, and for the right price to top it off. As he exited the store he knew that he had purchased the guitar on his own. As he was driving away with the new purchase in hand, he felt as though he was being watched from above. He kept on driving. As he proceeded home he began to rationalize his actions comforting himself with the thought that once he played the guitar everything would be fine. Within minutes he arrived home and unpacked the guitar. Oops. He forgot to buy the cable needed to connect the guitar to the amp. Now, instead of playing the guitar and feeling better about everything, he needed to go back to the store to get the necessary cable. The only problem was he knew if he went back to the same store the Lord would make him return the guitar. So off he went to another store, except that store did not have the cable he needed. So he moved on to another. He told himself that if the second store did not have the cable, he would just go back home. As it turned out, the second store did not have the cable either. But as he walked out of the second store he waivered on his commitment to return home. As he walked to his vehicle a man began approaching the young man, trying to gain his attention. The young man turned his attention to the man as he came closer. When the man came within a few feet he began speaking to the young man of a coin he had found. He asked the young man if he wanted to guess what side the coin would land on if the man flipped the coin. The young man then realized that the coin flip presented a probability of danger. The young man then immediately understood that he had been flipping that coin the whole day. All of the sudden the man turned and walked away as if summoned to do so. At that moment the young man repented to the Lord, got into his vehicle and returned the guitar to the store. Whether or not you see it yet, this is a typical example of confusion, its cause, its effect and its cure.

Let us begin by making clear that God is not confused. But He does bring and cause confusion. God employs, sends, and uses confusion for His purposes (Isaiah 22:5) (For more on this topic read *The War of the Lord*). It, like all things, originates from Him, not another source.
For example, consider:

- Where God saw the evil intent of men's hearts and purposed to come down and confuse the language of man, *"so that they will not understand one another's speech."* So *"the Lord confused the language of the whole earth; and from there the*

Lord scattered them abroad over the face of the whole earth" (Genesis 11:6-9); or

- When the Lord led His people out of Egypt and Pharaoh followed in pursuit that "*the Lord looked down on the army of the Egyptians through the pillar of fire and cloud and brought the army of the Egyptians into confusion. He caused their chariot wheels to swerve, and He made them drive with difficulty; so the Egyptians said, "Let us flee from Israel, for the Lord is fighting for them against the Egyptians*" (Exodus 14:24-25); or

- When the Lord spoke to Moses about the inhabitants of the land to which the Lord was bringing His people, and the Lord said, "*I will send My terror ahead of you, and throw into confusion all the people among whom you come, and I will make all your enemies turn their backs to you*" (Exodus 23:27; Deuteronomy 7:23); or

- When Moses spoke to the sons of Israel with regard to their potential disobedience or forsaking of the Lord, and he warned them that the Lord, in such an instance, would send upon them curses, *confusion*, and rebuke (Deuteronomy 28:20); or

- When Gideon and his 300 blew their trumpets near the camp of Midian as commanded by the Lord, and the Lord caused the Midianites to set their swords, one against another and caused the whole army to flee (Judges 7:22-23); or

- When the Ashdodites and the Ekronites captured the ark of the Lord, and He brought against them and their cities, great and deadly confusion (1 Sam. 5:6-12); or

- When Paul set free a slave-girl from an evil spirit and as a result the whole city was thrown into confusion (Acts 16:16-20); or

- When Ephesus was filled with confusion at the preaching of the gospel (Acts 19:29, 32).

As with many of these examples, it is not uncommon for both situations (confusion and no confusion) to occur simultaneously out of the same event, like on the day of Pentecost. The Bible makes it clear that the disciples were gathered together in one place and in one accord, in obedience to the Lord's instruction. There was no confusion in the gathering. Then suddenly the Holy Spirit fell upon them and they all began speaking in languages not their own. Others, who were among them, but not of them, described those that gathered as acting drunk or (confused). Peter, understanding what the crowd of unbelievers saw, stood up and said, *"These men are not drunk, as you suppose"* (Acts 2:15). In a single instance you have those who were not confused and those who were confused or saw confusion. The first point here is that it is wrong and dangerous to believe that God does not confuse. The second point is that confusion does not occur in or to those wholly given over to the Father's will. But by and through them, confusion can come to those who are living in opposition to His will. I will speak more on that in a second.

One other thing to note here; there has been no evidence provided that suggests that Satan orchestrated, directed, or caused confusion at any point in human history. That is because there is none. The belief that confusion is a work of the devil is completely unsupported by Scripture and is simply man's attempt to disregard the things of God and avoid God's ways, by calling evil what is good and good what is evil.

As for what confusion is, it is simply an attribute of sinfulness. God utilizes confusion as the evidence of sin. Where there is no sin, there is no confusion. Where there is sin, there you will also find confusion (Isaiah 9:13, 16). Confusion does not cause sin. It is the evidence of sin. Much like smoke to a fire or fever to an infection; fever does not cause infection, nor does smoke cause a fire, but is the evidence of it.

Take for example the church at Corinth where confusion reigned. The First Letter to the Corinthians was not Paul's first encounter with them. He had instructed them previously about many things, yet they remained confused and spiritually immature (1 Corinthians 1:16-17; 3:1-3). Paul addresses their confusion by rebuking them for their fleshliness, immaturity, and quarreling as seen in everything from: claiming allegiance to certain men, as opposed to Christ (1 Corinthians 1:11-13); allowing sexual immorality to persist in the church (5:1-2); and fighting over who or what in the church was more spiritual (Chapters 12-14). There was confusion in Corinth. The confusion was not the source of the sin, but the evidence of it. The source of the sin was the evil desires within their hearts (Mark 7:20-23).

Now let's revisit our young man from earlier to see if we can gain a more complete understanding of confusion. As we have learned, confusion is sent by God to show man something. If man sees that something he will do well. (Joshua 2) If man remains blind he will only find more trouble. (Genesis 4:1-12)

Therefore, the cause of confusion is sin, more specifically, the lack of finding satisfaction in hearing and obeying the word of the Lord. The effects of confusion are giving up or losing the word that the Lord has spoken, followed by a dulling of spiritual vision allowing the confused person to walk farther away from Truth. The cure to confusion is always and only repentance. Without repentance, confusion only grows into deception, lies, sin, and death.

Our young man had a desire in his heart. There was something that he wanted. He never surrendered that desire to the Lord to see if it was the Lord's desire. He kept it as his own. The Lord then spoke to our young man. Now his desire was in opposition to the Lord's words. Yet, he held on to the desire instead of releasing it to God. (Sin). Then confusion began to set in. He began to defend and justify his desire to himself and to God. Then at some point he completely disregarded the Lord's command. He wanted his desire and he got it. However, in this case, the Lord's mercy continued and He revealed the reality of the events of the day to our young man through the actions of the man in the parking lot. Finally, our young man's eyes were opened. He repented in his heart. Confusion left and he turned his heart repentance into action and returned the guitar to the store. Thank the Lord for His mercy, but do not make the mistake of assuming it will always be there for you.

So as you can see, desire found in the heart of man, not surrendered to God, will lead to frustration and discontentment that will lead to confusion. The confusion only highlights the previous failure to surrender to God. If there is no repentance, then confusion will increase, only leading to more trouble. It can continue to the point of no return. However, if there is repentance, then the confusion is diminished and right-standing with the Lord returns.

I pray that your understanding of confusion has changed and you now see that it is not an attack from Satan but a sign from God. Recognize it and repent. Now, if you are carnally-minded and not inclined to appraise all things spiritually, then you have already reasoned in your mind that not all confusion has a spiritual connection or is orchestrated by God. In other words, you are thinking of the countless things in everyday life that are confusing; like learning algebra or how to play a musical instrument, and those have nothing to do with God. That is where you are gravely mistaken.

In those times, the confusion need not be directly related to sin, but it is in those seemingly non-spiritual times of confusion where we learn to employ the ways of man instead of the ways of God in dealing with the confusion. One example would be to deal with confusion by acquiring information, as in the case of understanding algebra. Another would be to practice a skill so as to eliminate the confusion, as in the case of learning to play the flute. Each time we learn to deal with our confusion in this way we step further and further away from the way of the Lord in His dealings with man and his sinfulness. With God, confusion is not eliminated by information or practice, but repentance and surrender. If we grow to understand confusion as not being a spiritual attribute, we create a barrier to our own repentance. Eventually, you will find yourself doing what you know to be wrong and even hate; all because of unabated confusion.

Chapter 10

The Divine Intention -

A Journey to...

Salvation

The Obvious and the
Not so Obvious

Scripture Reading:

> *"For God so loved the world, that He gave His only begotten Son, that whoever believes in Him shall not perish, but have eternal life. For God did not send the Son into the world to judge the world, but that the world might be saved through Him"* (John 3:16-17).

"[God] desires all men to be saved and to come to the knowledge of the truth" (1 Timothy 2:4).

Our two Scripture readings provide us a glimpse into the Divine Intention. The heart intention of God is none other than the salvation of man. The plan and purpose of the salvation of man was <u>not</u> a consequence of Adam and Eve's sin. On the contrary, the creation of man and man's subsequent failure was a necessary part of the Divine Intention (Genesis 3:21)(see also Eyes to See – Garments of Skin). As we learn from Ephesians, the Lord God chose man in Christ before the foundation of the world, that man would be reconciled to Him (1:4). Before Adam, before sin, God predestined that He would have sons through His Son (Hebrew 4:3b). This was and is His will (Ephesians 1:5). The Lord God ordained that man would be redeemed from the place of separation from God through God Himself, in and through the Person of His Son, Jesus; and that by the shedding of His blood (v. 7). In His wisdom God made known to man this plan - His will for the salvation of man. He revealed the Divine Intention with a view towards the fulfillment of His purpose, that being, the summing up of all things in Christ, His Son (v. 8-10).

His plan was first revealed to Abram as recorded in Genesis 12 (see also Galatians 3:8-9). Abram was seventy-five years old when he was commanded by God to *leave the land of his birth* and to *leave his relatives* and *his father's house* and *go to a land that the Lord God would show him* and *in that place, the Lord God would make him a great nation* and *would bless him* (Genesis 12:1-2). In

His wisdom God was communicating to man the journey to eternal fellowship with Himself; the journey to salvation. Abram did not see it in the natural, but he believed Him nonetheless. By faith Abram obeyed by going to a land that was not his own, so that in that new land he could receive an inheritance, not from his ancestors, but from God (Hebrews 11:8-10).

Upon arriving in the land, the Lord said to Abram, "*to your descendants I give this land*" (Genesis 12:7; 15:18). When the Lord spoke these words to Abram it was impossible for those words to be true, but for God (Luke 18:27). To begin with, the Canaanite and the Perizzite were dwelling then in the land that the Lord had promised (Genesis 13:7). Moreover, when God spoke His promise to Abram, Abram had no descendants and presumably no manner of having descendants. He had neither a descendant in the flesh (Isaac) (Genesis 15:4; 21:7; 22:2) nor a descendant in the spirit (those of faith) (Romans 4:16; Galatians 3:7). Yet, it was to these descendants that the covenant of God would be manifested. (Deuteronomy 1:6-8; Galatians 3:9, 14, 29)

Then when Abram was ninety-nine years old the Lord confirmed His promise saying to Abram,

"Walk before Me, and be blameless. I will establish My covenant between Me and you, and I will multiply you exceedingly.... and I will make nations of you, and kings will come forth from you.... and I will give to you and to your descendants after you, the land of your sojournings, all the land of Canaan, for an everlasting

possession; and I will be their God" (Genesis 17:1-2, 6, 8).

Abraham's (Genesis 17:5) descendants in the flesh, as promised by the Lord, were the sons of Israel (Hebrews 7:5). The first of these descendants was Isaac who was born to Abraham and Sarah by the word of the Lord (Genesis 18:10). Here again we get a revelation and hopefully a further understanding into the Divine Intention. Firstly, God allows man to realize that His promises are impossible to obtain without God Himself (Genesis 15:1-3) and secondly, that the way God chooses to reveal His plan through the circumstances of man's existence are but a means to an end, and not an end in themselves (Isaiah 55:8-9).

In other words, it is meant for man to understand that there is an eternal purpose in all that God does. That eternal purpose is hidden from man (John 13:7; Luke 9:44-45; 24:44-45). The natural man may observe activities within the temporal world and he may even participate in those activities, but the eternal purpose behind those activities is not known to him. Only the man in whom the Spirit of God freely operates can know and comprehend the activities of God in the world, by what he observes or lives. According to Psalm 103, Moses was such a man. Moses knew the ways of God. He knew the eternal purposes that lied behind all that God was doing in Egypt and in the years of wandering in the wilderness. On the other hand, those Divine purposes were not so obvious to the people he led out of Egypt even though they observed the same activities (v.7) (see Exodus 7-11).

The man not surrendered to the Lord operates from a face-value paradigm. He observes his surroundings at a surface level and from there he makes determinations and judgments (Matthew 14:17; 15:33; Mark 9:5; John 11:8, 16). He usually finds his satisfaction or dissatisfaction in what he has observed with his natural senses. However, as we will see, God always has a Divine intention that lies behind all that is observed at face-value. What the natural man sees as finished or impossible, God sees as the progression towards His purpose (John 11:14-15).

This simple truth about God's way is revealed to us again through the life of Abraham. At 100 years old, finally having a child, an heir, is a big deal. There is much reason to celebrate. But a very short time later (approximately 15-20 years) God commands Abraham to offer Isaac as a sacrifice to Him (Genesis 22:2). God, in essence says to Abraham, *"Yes, I promised you a child, an heir, and yes an heir was born to you. However, the birth of the child was not the end; it was the means; the means to an eternal purpose."* God's eternal purpose in giving Abraham and Sarah a child was to see if Abraham feared God and to reveal Himself as Jehovah Jireh. When Abraham did not withhold his son from God but trusted that He would provide for Himself an acceptable offering, Abraham proved His fear of the Lord and now *knew* God as Jehovah Jireh (v. 8, 11-13). Through Abraham's faith, man would know truth - *the Lord Will Provide* (v. 14).

Do you not think there were times during those years that Abraham found complete satisfaction in what the Lord had given when he watched Isaac growing, learning, and playing? But God had far more to give; far more than was given at the first; far more than Abraham could see with his natural eyes. Abraham needed to look beyond the obvious and take personal ownership of the not so obvious. He needed to surrender to God and His purpose and to trust Him when He spoke. Abraham did so, and for that he is called the father of our faith (Genesis 22:11-12; Romans 4:16).

Now Isaac became the father of Jacob (whose name was changed to Israel as recorded in Genesis 32:28), who in turn became the father of twelve sons. These twelve sons became the namesakes for the twelve tribes of the sons of Israel (Genesis 49:1-28) and they and their descendants would ultimately find themselves as slaves in Egypt, until God through His servant Moses, in the fourth generation from Abraham (Genesis 15:16) delivered the sons of Israel from their oppressor (Exodus 3:7-9; 12:37-41).

Now it was from the oppressed condition of the sons of Israel that the Lord would further reveal His Divine Intention. At that time the Lord spoke to Moses on Horeb, the mountain of God saying,

"*I have surely seen the affliction of My people who are in Egypt, and have given heed to their cry because of their taskmasters, for I am aware of their sufferings. So I have come down to deliver them from the power of the Egyptians, and to bring them up from that land to a good and spacious land, to a land flowing with milk and honey, to the place of the Canaanite and the Hittite and the Amorite and the Perizzite and the Hivite and the Jebusite"* (Exodus 3:7-8).

To Moses, God is communicating the fullness of His intention to *come down* (John 3:16) Himself and deliver or redeem man from his fallen condition (Romans 3:23; 5:12) and then bring that redeemed man *up to a land* that God Himself has prepared for man and where God Himself abides (Exodus 23:20; 29:45; John 3:17; Romans 6:23). *"Up to the place that He has prepared for man"* is synonymous with both the land promised to Abram as recorded in Genesis 12:7 and the eternal life promised by Jesus (John 14:1-6; 1 John 2:25) and confirmed in the messages of Paul to the churches (Ephesians 2:4-6; Colossians 3:4; 1 Thessalonians 5:10; 2 Timothy 2:11-12).

After speaking to Moses on Horeb, God then sent him back to Egypt to bring the sons of Israel out of bondage – to commence the journey to the Divine Intention (Exodus 3:7). However, Pharaoh's heart was hardened and he refused to release Israel to Moses (Exodus 5:1-2; 11:9-10). Then on the evening before they left out of Egypt, the evening thereafter known as the Passover (Luke 22:1), God instructed Moses to have every household of the sons of Israel kill a one-year old unblemished lamb. Each household was to take some of the blood from the lamb and put it on the doorposts and lintel of the house. The lamb was then to be roasted and consumed by those present. Moses then instructed them as to the Feast of Unleavened Bread which was to be celebrated annually from generation to generation as a memorial to how the Lord took the sons of Israel out of Egypt (Exodus 12).

Both the Passover with its shed blood and the memorial feast with its unleavened bread represented the life and ministry of Jesus on the earth (John 1:36; Hebrews 4:15). That very night, after the Lord executed His final judgment against all the firstborn of Egypt, Pharaoh relented and released the people to Moses (Exodus 12:29-34). The following morning God, through Moses, led Israel out of Egyptian bondage (Numbers 33:3-4).

The very day that they set out God commanded that Moses sanctify all of the firstborn of Israel, both of man and beast saying,

"*It belongs to Me*" (Exodus 13:1-2).

Moses did as the Lord commanded and he further commanded that the people "*should eat no leaven*" (v. 3). Then the people set out from Egypt and "*the Lord was going before them in a pillar of cloud by day to lead them on the way, and in a pillar of fire by night to give them light, that they might travel by day and by night. He did not take away the pillar of cloud by day, nor the pillar of fire by night, from before the people* (v. 20-22).

The journey to the Intention of God had begun in earnest. As He had spoken to Moses, God came down and delivered the sons of Israel from the power of the Egyptians and now He was leading them to the land which He had promised to Abraham; the land that He would give to Abraham's descendants as an inheritance.

Before we move on in our recounting of the journey to the Lord's Intention, it must be understood that it was no small thing that the first order of business as the journey commenced was that the firstborn of Israel were to be sanctified. The sanctification of the firstborn represented giving all to the Lord. The journey requires sanctification. It requires that those that take the journey belong to the Lord. It also requires complete surrender. At the outset of the journey God commanded sanctification. That sanctification was accomplished by a giving of the firstborn. On the surface it appears that God is only requiring a beginning portion when in fact He is requiring all. To give the first meant to give all. The first represented all that came after. It is a mistake to believe that the first represents only a beginning portion.

Take Abraham for example. He gave his firstborn, his only. When he gave his firstborn to God at Mount Moriah, he gave to God all that that firstborn represented; his inheritance from God. He gave it all, and all that God promised him he received in return. Even with God Himself we see the truth of the firstborn. God gave His first to man; His only begotten Son. He gave His all. By giving His Son to the world, He received all that came after; sons by adoption – The Divine Intention. To give your firstborn is to give all that follows after, because the inheritance is tied to the firstborn. This is the significance of God's judgment on the firstborn of Egypt. It was a judgment on all, not just a beginning portion.

In addition to the sanctification, Moses commanded that the sons of Israel "should eat no leaven." Throughout Scripture, when the Lord forbade the use of or warned of leaven, that leaven always referred to sin (Matthew 4:1-2; 16:6-12; Mark 6:14-29; 8:15; Luke 12:1; 1 Corinthians

5:8). It was in that vein that Moses commanded that the people, as they began their journey, should eat no leaven.

Up to this point everything appeared to be moving along smoothly. God communicated His plan. Now that plan was taking shape. The next step in the plan is to advance to the intended destination. So God leads the people out and the first place He brings them is to the Red Sea (Exodus 13:18). At this point Pharaoh has changed his mind about letting Israel go and has vowed to return them to Egypt as slaves (14:5-9). With the sea in front of them and Pharaoh behind, the people became frightened and accused Moses [and God] of leading them into the wilderness to die there, reminding Moses that while still in Egypt they asked him to leave them alone that they "may serve the Egyptians" (14:10-12).

How quickly the sons of Israel forgot how with a powerful hand the Lord brought them out of Egypt (Exodus 13:16). Nevertheless, with great power God delivered Israel from Pharaoh's pursuit, utterly destroying Pharaoh's army in the process (Exodus 14:26-31). The Lord continued to lead Israel through the wilderness, all the while providing them with protection, food and water (Exodus 15:19, 22-25; 16:4-5; 17:1-16). Within the span of several weeks, Israel was no longer gathering hay and making bricks. There was no more waking up to the cracking of an Egyptian whip or the threat of death from exhaustion. After plundering Egypt of its wealth, the people were freed from the strong hand of Pharaoh (Exodus 12:51). Yet, at every turn, the sons of Israel found reason to grumble and complain against the Lord (Exodus 14:10-12; 16:3; 17:2-3).

Despite their continued grumbling and complaining the Lord led the sons of Israel to the edge of the land of their inheritance. It was then that He commanded that they go in and take the land (Exodus 33:1-3). The Divine Intention was nearing its completion. So in the fourteenth month after leaving Egypt, sons of Israel departed from Mount Sinai where the Lord met with Moses and they settled in the wilderness of Paran (Numbers 10:11-13). Then from the wilderness of Paran, Moses sent twelve spies into Canaan to spy out the land (Numbers 13:17-20). After spending forty days in the land of promise the twelve men returned to report what they had found. Ten of them reported that the land was indeed flowing with milk and honey and had fruit as never before seen. But also, that the land was inhabited by giants who lived in fortified cities and that the sons of Israel became like grasshoppers in their sight (Number 13:27-28, 33). Despite Caleb's [an 11th spy] plea that they would surely overcome nonetheless, the sons of Israel rebelled against Moses, Aaron, Joshua and Caleb and spoke among themselves of appointing a leader and returning to Egypt (Number 14:4).

When the Lord heard their complaints He said to the sons of Israel,

"Your corpses will fall in this wilderness, even all your numbered men, according to your complete number from twenty years old and upward, who have grumbled against Me. Surely you shall not come into the land in which I swore to settle you, except [Caleb and Joshua]. Your children, however…. I will bring them in, and they

will know the land which you have rejected. But as for you, your corpses will fall in this wilderness. Your sons shall be shepherds for forty years in the wilderness, and they will suffer for your unfaithfulness, until your corpses lie in the wilderness. According to the number of days which you spied out the land, forty days, for every day you shall bear your guilt a year" (Numbers 14:29-34).

As for the ten spies who made the whole congregation grumble against the Lord by bringing out a bad report concerning the land; they died by a plague before the Lord (14:36-37).

As we learned from the Lord's command to Moses on the day Israel came out of Egypt, the journey requires that those that take the journey belong to the Lord completely. We can see now what the Lord meant. Even though these people were called by God and protected by the blood of the lamb while in Egypt, the fact that they refused to thereafter sanctify their hearts so as to completely belong to the Lord kept them from the Divine Intention and subjected them to the wrath of God.

So the Lord then commanded Moses to turn the people away from Canaan and return to the wilderness (Deuteronomy 2:1; Numbers 14:25). There they would wander for forty years until the number of them that rejected the Divine Intention had died (Deuteronomy 2:14-15). After the time of judgment had passed, the Lord directed them back to the edge of the land of His Intention and commanded that they begin to occupy and possess the land. Moses then led them in the conquest of the two kings of the Amorites until the Lord led Israel to the place just beyond the Jordan (Deuteronomy 2:16-18, 31-36; 3:1-10). At that place the Lord told Moses to look upon the land, but that he would not enter because he *"did not treat the Lord as holy in the sight of the sons of Israel"* when the Lord commanded him to speak to the rock in the wilderness of Zin. Moses was then instructed to commission Joshua to lead the sons of Israel across the Jordan and into the land that the Lord had promised to Abraham (Deuteronomy 3:26-28; Numbers 20:1, 12).

So under the leadership of Joshua, the people crossed the Jordan opposite Jericho into the land (Joshua 1:1-4; 3:16). While the sons of Israel camped in the land they observed the Passover (Joshua 5:10). On the day after the Passover, they ate some of the produce of the land, unleavened cakes and parched grain. The manna that they had been eating throughout the journey ceased on the day after they had eaten some of the produce of the land, *"so that the sons of Israel no longer had manna, but they ate some of the yield of the land of Canaan"* (Joshua 5:11-12). Joshua would then lead the sons of Israel through the land conquering until such time that the sons of Israel divided the land among themselves (Joshua 13). The Divine Intention was complete. But the tragedy was that except for two men, none of those that left Egypt entered the land of promise (Deuteronomy 1:34-40; Exodus 12:37; Numbers 14:28-32; Joshua 5:2-7).

In and through the circumstances of their existence God revealed His whole plan of salvation for mankind. God's purpose for this people was right there before them. Israel's forty years of wandering in the desert was due primarily to their unwillingness to look beyond the obvious [self] and take personal ownership of the not so obvious [the Divine Intention]. True, they were no longer within the grasp of Pharaoh's harsh rule. God heard their cry. He delivered them! But leaving Egypt was only the beginning of a Divine purpose. Redeeming them from their oppressors was only a necessary step to get them to the land that God had prepared for them. The Intention was the land of promise and what it meant to enter in there (Exodus 29:45; John 14:3). The goal had yet to be accomplished.

The sons of Israel failed to take their eyes off of themselves and their desires and look instead to the Lord and to His Intention. Even *before* their deliverance from Egypt and a generation of wandering in the wilderness, there was no indication that this people possessed as their own, understood or was even interested in the Intention of the Lord. Their cries while in Egypt, the cries to God about their hardships and oppressions, were about their conditions while living in Egypt, not about the fact that they were even there in the first place. It is likely that their cry was, *"Lord, make it like it was in the days of Joseph, when we were blessed in this place. The Egyptian king who knew us and showed us favor is now dead and the present one does not know us. Lord, help us."*

This statement is supported by a complete absence of any statement directed to God or Moses by the sons of Israel *during* their wilderness experience requesting to advance quickly to the land of promise. We are able to refer to countless instances when they demanded or requested to return to Egypt, but not one demand or request to enter Canaan (see Exodus 14:10-12; 16:3;17:2-3; Numbers 11:4-6; 14:2-4; 16:12-14; 20:3-5)(but see Deuteronomy 1:41-46). God's purpose for this people and for man was made known to Israel. But in their sinful condition, they did not see it. It never entered their heart. This is made clear from the words of the Lord through the prophet Jeremiah some 800 years later when He said,

> *22 In the day that I brought them out of the land of Egypt, 24...they did not listen to Me, 26...and they did more evil than their fathers. 32 "Therefore, behold, days are coming," declares the Lord, 33"when ....the dead bodies of this people will be food for the birds of the sky and for the beasts of the earth* (Jeremiah 7:21-33).

In spite of being delivered from generations of death and slavery, and despite being covered by the blood of the lamb during the Lord's judgment upon Egypt, at every turn Israel refused to harken unto the voice of the Lord. Israel failed to hear and understand the whole work of God – His Divine Intention.

Wrath or Rest

So the question then becomes not what is God speaking or doing, but how is man responding (Genesis 22:18)? As it relates to the Divine Intention, there is much for us to learn from those who were delivered from Egypt. As we have just seen, they all fell in the wilderness because the word they heard [God's covenant with Abraham/the Divine Intention] did not profit them, because it was not united by faith (Hebrews 3:17; 4:2). We are warned not to follow their example of unbelief and disobedience, so as to face the wrath of God (3:12, 18-19; 4:6). The danger we encounter today is, like the sons of Israel, never possessing in our heart the heart Intention of the Lord – to bring us to the land that He has prepared. One of Israel's greatest errors was to not understand that the Divine Intention is a journey and not an overnight rescue. The oppressed sons of Israel were all on board to get out of work for a week or two to go up to the mountain and worship God (Exodus 5:3). But not one of them, save a few were ready to die to everything that they were and everything that they knew and allow a God who they hardly knew lead them through and to an unknown wilderness (Exodus 14:9-12). But that is exactly what God had intended and it is exactly what He did.

Our challenge is whether or not we will walk in step (obedience) with the Divine Intention. Therefore, "while a promise remains of entering His rest" (Hebrews 4:1) let us examine ourselves to see whether we are in the faith (2 Corinthians 13:5). In doing so, we have an advantage today that the early church did not have. They had the example of the sons of Israel from which to learn. On the other hand, we have the early church in addition to the sons of Israel.

Following Pentecost, the church struggled with the same temptations as did the sons of Israel. While a majority of Christians today believe that the early church had it right, the reality is that within several years of Pentecost, confusion and sin set in (Acts 15:1-12;

19:9;21:17-28; Galatians 2:11-16) and by the time Paul is writing his letters, the churches are in a very discouraging state. In examining their struggles we can better identify our true condition in relationship to the Divine Intention.

Like their brethren before them, the early church did not appreciate the fullness of God's Intention. The earliest Christians were satisfied in the redemptive work of the cross in the same way that the sons of Israel found satisfaction in the redemptive work of the Passover. The first Christians failed to understand the Lord when He told them that He was leading a journey, like when He said to them time after time, "*Follow Me*" or when He said,

"*I am the way, and the truth, and the life; no one comes to the Father but through Me*" (John 14:6).

It is clear by His words that there was a journey involved and that the journey required leaving one place and going to another. The "one" place was [Egypt] the life of self and sin. The "other" place was the *destination* – the Father. And there is only one *way* to arrive at that destination – Jesus. We can see in the New Testament writings of the Apostles that those that were baptized into this way were not so much aware of what that baptism represented, not unlike the sons of Israel coming out of Egypt after partaking of the Passover meal. To most if not all, their baptism accomplished something, instead of representing something that should be.

Paul, in writing primarily to Christians of his day, admonished them not to stop at the redemptive work.

The focus in each of his letters was leading the church to sanctification in Christ; to a death of oneself and a complete surrender to God much like that that God required of the sons of Israel upon leaving Egypt. He warned them against trying to live a life [free from Egypt], but not sanctified to or led by God (Romans 6:2, 8, 12-13; see also Exodus 13).

Take for example the Letter to the Galatians. In that letter Paul explains that, "*as long as the heir is a child, he does not differ at all from a slave although he is owner of everything*" (Galatians 4:1). Paul beseeched the church to stay in the truth *until Christ is formed in them*, lest his labors concerning them would be found to be in vain (4:11, 19). Paul was laboring to bring these who were justified to the place of sonship through Christ. We find also in his letters to the churches at Corinth, Colossae, and Ephesus that Paul labored to bring those who were justified to maturity in Christ (Ephesians 4:13). In those churches sin remained despite the work of the cross (1 Corinthians 3:1-3; Colossians 3:3-9; Ephesians 4:17-32). Paul reproves the churches to live no longer as "fleshly men" or "in the world." Paul entreated them to "*put on the new self, which in the likeness of God has been created in righteousness and holiness of the truth*" (Ephesians 4:24) and to "*set their minds on the things above, not on the things that are on earth*" (Colossians 3:2) striving to "*walk in a manner worthy of the Lord*" (Colossians 1:10).

And even though he is not addressing specific sin in the churches at Philippi or Rome, Paul nonetheless instructs those that believed "*not to be conformed to this world*" (Romans 12:2). He instructs that they "*abhor what is evil and cling to what is good*" (v.9) and to practice what is "*true*" and "*pure*" (Philippians 4:8). He like the other apostles understood that being justified by the cross of Christ, although absolutely necessary, was not the end of God's intention.

Peter and James for example, each write letters to teach and to encourage those who have believed in Jesus to be filled to overflowing with joy at every trial, understanding that the trial is but a test of one's faith in Christ which produces endurance that results in perfection, completeness, and wholeness or as Peter writes, results in "*the salvation of your soul*" (James 1:2-3; 1 Peter 1:6-9).

We know that "*all those who came out of Egypt led by Moses*" failed to enter into the Lord's Rest because of their disobedience (Hebrews 3:16-18). In light of what we have seen about the early church, we have to wonder whether or not most of them failed as well. Remember, Paul writes to Timothy towards the end of Paul's ministry informing him "*that all who are in Asia have turned away from me*" (2 Timothy 1:15) and that even his co-laborer, Demas deserted him "*having loved this present world*" (2 Timothy 4:10). Was Paul's despair and concern over the spiritual condition of those that professed the cross of Christ well-founded? It was well-founded if the churches continued in their fleshliness and refused to repent. Now the toughest question is are the Apostles' words written to us? Are we stubbornly going along the same path as those who came before us? Or do we arrogantly think we are different? Are we heading for His rest or His wrath?

We must heed the words of God. Abraham's descendants in the spirit are all who by faith believe the word of the Lord. We must learn from the example of those that came before us. We cannot repeat their mistakes. We cannot mistake a part of the work of God as the whole work of God. It is that mistake that has left many a "Christian" on the outside looking in when it comes to heaven (Matthew 7:21-23).

When we examine the Christian faith of our time, we are challenged to deny the overwhelming message of salvation. This Christian salvation theology is propagated at every Christian gathering and in every Christian message, whether it is spoken, sung or written and it could not be further from the truth. It has in fact prevented most sinners from truly surrendering to God. The single greatest danger facing the Christian today is not religious, political, or financial persecution [Egyptian oppression]. It is not that evil, over-reaching government [Pharaoh]. And certainly it is not Satan, humanism or even Islam [the Hittite, the Perizzite, the Amorite, the Canaanite and the Jebusite]. No, the single greatest danger for today's Christian is the belief that he or she *is saved* [Partook of the Passover Lamb and covered by the Passover blood]. Many Christians believe and teach that if they accept Jesus Christ as savior, they *are* saved. The sons of Israel found this to be false the hard way.

Today's Christian leadership has now for decades sold to the willing masses the theology that accepting Christ, by confessing Him as Lord provides you with salvation and with this salvation, you have guaranteed entrance into heaven. One very popular preaching line of today is

"Christ has died for you." It is not even implied, but the next line is, *"so you don't have to."* Then the hearers go on living their merry lives until.... This fleshly theology bars the work of sanctification in the lives of those who hear it and it is dangerously similar to the attitude and words of Korah when he accused Moses of exalting himself *"above the assembly of the Lord"* (Numbers 16:3). Korah and others rose up against Moses telling him he had gone far enough, *"for all the congregation are holy, every one of them, and the Lord is in their midst"* (16:3). When the Holy Spirit, like Moses, comes along and deals with sin in our lives, we like Korah, declare, "Enough! We are holy." You may not say the words, but you possess the attitude. The danger is you may not see it until it is too late.

Unlike today's Christian leaders, the Apostles understood and taught that being redeemed, reconciled, justified, and freed from sin, did not equate to you being saved. None of the Apostles led the Redeemed to believe that they had obtained salvation, or in other words reached the end of the Divine Intention. On the contrary, each warned believers not to stagnate in their profession of faith, and they labored to bring the Justified to salvation through the sanctifying work of the Holy Spirit (Romans 6:19; 1 Thessalonians 4:1, 3, 7; 2 Thessalonians 2:13; 1 Peter 1:2; James 5:7-11; 1 John 3:7-10).

We have witnessed with the sons of Israel, that the Divine Intention came to a completion after a journey led by God. To teach and to preach that it is anything prior to that is to teach and to preach lies and deception - that sanctification and a sinless life is extreme and unnecessary.

The Scriptural evidence of the salvation of man being the Divine Intention and that the Divine Intention is a journey is overwhelming. Take for example the words from Romans 6:22,

> "...now having been freed from sin and enslaved to God, you derive your benefit, resulting in sanctification, and the outcome, eternal life."

And again from 2 Thessalonians 2:13,

> "But we should always give thanks to God for you, brethren beloved by the Lord, because God has chosen you from the beginning for salvation through sanctification by the Spirit and faith in the truth."

And there are still others like: Acts 26:18 ("*that they may receive forgiveness of sins and an inheritance among those who have been sanctified by faith in Me*"); Romans 13:11 ("*...for now salvation is nearer to us than when we believed*"); Philippians 2:12 ("*work out your salvation with fear and trembling*"); 1 Timothy 4:16 ("*Persevere in these things, for as you do this you will ensure salvation both for yourself and for those who hear you*"); 1 Peter 1:5 ("*for a salvation ready to be revealed in the last time*"); and 1 Peter 2:1-3 ("*Therefore, putting aside all malice and all deceit and hypocrisy and envy and all slander, like newborn babies, long for the pure milk of the word, so that by it you may grow in respect to salvation, if you have tasted the kindness of the Lord*"). The message in these verses is that salvation is the Destination, not the dawning.

To understand salvation, you must understand the purpose of salvation. You must understand from what are you saved? As Romans 5:9-10 tells us, if we are to be saved, it will be from the wrath of God (see also 1 Thessalonians 1:10; 5:9). The sons of Israel learned that lesson. People who proclaim that they **are** saved do not yet have a revelation of the Divine Intention. Salvation is for a time yet to come, referred to in the Bible as "until the end" or "the day of the Lord" (see 1 Peter 1:5). In other words, a person who is still on the temporal side of the grave, having yet to stand before the Lord in judgment cannot proclaim the fact of their salvation, but only a hope in it.

Have we convinced ourselves today that we are something or someone who we are not? Has our theology blinded us to our condition? Are we like the sons of Israel in Egypt and the early church that gladly accepted the work of the cross but remained in sin, never even interested in the heart Intention of God?

Because our deception is clothed in terms of "salvation" it will be very difficult to die to that as the evidence of who we are. It happened the same way in Egypt. You left Egypt if you were a son of Israel. Once you left Egypt, it did not matter whether or not you were a son of Israel. Just ask Korah and Dathan. The fact that you are a son of Israel means nothing to God once you leave Egypt. If you do not sanctify yourself to God and follow Him, your identity will not save you from His wrath. The same is true today for those who are trusting in their "salvation" identity.

While it is the desire of God that all men be saved, it is certain that far from all men will walk in step with the Divine Intention so as to inherit eternal life (Matthew 13:30, 41-43). In fact more will miss it than inherit it (Matthew 7:13-14). The reason for this is found in John 3:19 which states,

> "The Light has come into the world, and men loved the darkness rather than the Light, for their deeds were evil."

Will you love the darkness rather than the Light? Will you love the Light so as to follow It to the Divine Intention? Or will you prefer to remain in or return to the darkness? This is the lesson of this chapter. I pray we all learn it.

✦

Chapter 11

EYES TO SEE

As you read this chapter,

I pray that the eyes of your heart may be enlightened (Ephesians 1:18).

Scripture Reading: John 9

It is an underappreciated reality that man cannot see unless and until the Lord gives him sight (Deuteronomy 29:4). Without sight man understands and believes in God not as He really exists, but how man believes He exists; not as He is, but how man is. This truth is clearly seen in the account of Peter's revelation of the Christ. One day Jesus asked His disciples,

> *"Who do people say that the Son of Man is?" And they said, "Some say John the Baptist; and others, Elijah; but still others, Jeremiah, or one of the prophets." He said to them, "But who do you say that I am?" Simon Peter answered, "You are the Christ, the Son of the living God." And Jesus said to him, "Blessed are you, Simon Barjona, because flesh and blood did not reveal this to you, but My Father who is in heaven"* (Matthew 16:13-17).

As the disciples reported to Jesus, the people of their day believed Him to be someone other than whom He was. They believed Him to be someone they had a connection with; knowledge of; someone with whom they could relate. Opinions were formed and beliefs were established. Yet, there was no truth to any of them. The Truth stood before them; however He was hidden from their eyes. It was not until the Lord opened their eyes that the truth was known.

A similar experience occurred to the two men traveling the road to Emmaus. In that instance, the Lord hid Himself from their eyes until the appropriate time (Luke 24:16, 31). Still, until they were given sight, the

Truth was unknown to them. In the meantime, they had formed opinions and beliefs that were erroneous.

This reality is not limited to seeing and knowing the Person of God, but seeing and knowing all things concerning God. Jesus frequently taught in parables. Once, when His disciples asked Him about a parable, Jesus said,

> "To you has been given the mystery of the kingdom of God, but those who are outside get everything in parables, so that while seeing, they may see and not perceive, and while hearing, they may hear and not understand, otherwise they might return and be forgiven" (Mark 4:11-12).

Our dependency upon God for sight also applies to the daily activities of our lives (Matthew 16:5-12; John 11:11-15). Consider the life of Elisha. Elisha and his servant were being pursued by the king of Aram. The king became enraged when Elisha repeatedly warned the king of Israel of the battle plans of the king of Aram. Elisha was doing this by the Spirit of the Lord. The king of Aram sought to capture Elisha, so he sent his army to surround the city where Elisha was staying. The next morning the servant of Elisha had risen early and went outside. He saw the Arameans surrounding the city with horses and chariots. The servant said to his master, "What shall we do?" Elisha answered,

> "Do not fear, for those who are with us are more than those who are with them." Then Elisha prayed and said, "O Lord, I pray, open his eyes that he may see."

And the Lord opened the servant's eyes and he saw; and behold, the mountain was full of horses and chariots of fire all around Elisha" (2 Kings 6:16-17).

Now when the Arameans came to Elisha, he prayed to the Lord to strike them with blindness. The Lord blinded the Aramean army so that they did not recognize Elisha. Elisha then led them to Samaria, to the king of Israel. He then asked the Lord to open their eyes that they may see. The man of God then instructed the king of Israel not to harm the Arameans but to prepare a feast for them. Following the feast, the army returned to their king and never again returned to Israel (2 Kings 6:18-23).

And there are many more examples of sight being dependent upon God, like sight being given to Joseph and blindness to the wise men of Egypt (Genesis 41); sight given to Jeremiah and blindness to Zedekiah, king of Judah (2 Chronicles 36:11-21); and sight given to Daniel and blindness to the magicians and conjurers of Nebuchadnezzar (Daniel 2:19, 28). In each of these instances we are shown that despite what man may think that he knows, he knows nothing without revelation from God (see also Matthew 12:7; 16:17; 22:29-30).

For the remainder of this chapter I would like to share with you some of my experiences with this reality. There have been a number of instances over the past twenty years when the Lord spoke something to me, that until He spoke that thing, I was completely blind to the truth. Even though I may have held beliefs about what He was speaking, those beliefs and their corresponding actions in my life were not in agreement with the revelation I was presently receiving from Him. The following is some of what I saw:

Authority

All authority originates in God the Father, in whom inherent authority abides. He gives that authority to whomever He desires within His creation, whether it be to men, angels, or otherwise (Genesis 1:28 *man given authority over creation*; Exodus 7:1-2; Romans 13:1 *man given authority over man*; Job 1:12 *Satan given authority over man*; Job 39:19-20, 26-27; 40:15-24 *God giving authority to animals through their attributes*; John 8:28; Revelation 2:26-27 *The Father giving authority to His Son*). The Lord's giving of authority is never dependent upon a rank, title, or office (Jeremiah 1:5, 10; *Jeremiah, as a child, given the authority of prophet to destroy and to build nations and kingdoms*), although one in such a rank, title, or office can exercise authority when it is given by the Lord (2 Chronicles 7:17-20 *Solomon given authority to rule Israel*; Jeremiah 5:15-17 *Nebuchadnezzar given authority to overthrow Israel*; Luke 10:20 *the seventy given authority over the spirits*; John 19:8-11 *Pilate given authority over Jesus*). Authority is not a matter of privilege or right (John 3:1, 9-10 *Nicodemus, the teacher of Israel with no authority from God*). Apart from God there is no authority and the authority given only remains as long as He maintains it, and therefore, it is extrinsic to the one who receives it (1 Samuel 15:28 *King Saul stripped of his authority*). Authority is always transmitted by God speaking, either directly or indirectly to the recipient, (Isaiah 55:11; John 5:19; Matthew 28:18; John 16:13; Acts 6:8–7:53; 9:10-19; Job 2:6) and therefore it is interpersonal. Finally, the level of authority held is directly proportional to the revelation received (1 Kings 18:25-39; John 8:37-47 *no revelation equals no authority;* 1 Kings 18:36-38; Galatians 1:11 *much revelation equals much authority*).

I learned these truths from the Lord at a time when I was exercising a traditional pastoral authority over others. It was nothing extraordinary, simply a pastoral authority over members of a church congregation. In many ways it was expected by those who gave me such authority and accepted by those over whom I exercised that authority, yet I was exercising it at the command of man, not the Lord. In my exercising of that authority, part of what I did was to determine whether or not something to be spoken from among the congregation, as opposed to the pastoral staff, was from God. If I deemed it was not from God, then it was not to be shared publicly. I nearly always deemed it was not from God if I either did not fully understand it or if it spoke against the established church authority. If I understood what was offered or if it confirmed what was spoken by or believed by those in pastoral authority it was shared with all, after all, everything was to be done properly and orderly. At least so I believed.

But then the Holy Spirit spoke to me and said, "*Why are you stopping Me?*" He warned me of continuing in my way. With great conviction He made me to see the error and then said, "*If you continue in it, I will end you.*" You may not be able to appreciate the weight of the words He spoke, but I assure you, I have yet to hear anything in my life that stopped me in my tracks, as those words did. At that moment I repented of my sin and He was faithful to open my eyes to the truth.

For the very first time in my life I saw that there was no relationship between an office or position held and an authority given, especially my own. Prior to that time I always associated authority with a position or rank regardless of the environment. Within the religious context, I believed, if God was speaking, it was by and through the ministry leadership. It was not until the Lord gave me sight that I saw how wrong I was.

He opened my eyes to the truth found in the lives of Joseph, Gideon, David, and Jeremiah. Each of these men was called by God to exercise authority in his time. Each man exercised that authority as a result of hearing God speak. At the time God spoke, none held a position of power, influence, or authority; in fact, each held the lowest position available at the time. And the men over whom the authority was exercised did not hear God speak His authority to the one to whom the authority was given.

In the case of a seventeen year old Joseph, God spoke to him in dreams to the effect that his father, mother and older brothers would bow down to him and he would rule over them (Genesis 37:1-10). Despite their complete rejection of Joseph after sharing what the Lord showed him, a little more than twenty years later that is exactly what occurred as Joseph had risen to be governor in all of Egypt and his entire family came to Egypt from Canaan in search of food during a seven year famine. God, through a direct communication, established Joseph as the authority over his people and He did so even though Joseph was of no family rank when God first spoke to him (Genesis 41:46, 56-57; 42:1-2, 6) and He accomplished His will without consulting with or working through any then-existing authority figure in Joseph's life.

A little over four hundred years later following the death of Joshua, a generation arose in Israel who did not know the Lord or His works that He did for His people in Egypt (Judges 3:8, 10). As a result, Israel continually did evil in the sight of the Lord. So the Lord periodically delivered the sons of Israel over to their enemies (vv. 13-15). When they cried to the Lord on account of their oppressors, the Lord would raise up a judge who would deliver Israel from the hands of those who plundered them (v. 16). One of those judges was Gideon. Gideon was the youngest son of Joash the Abiezrite who was the least family in all Manasseh (6:11, 15).

In the days of Gideon the Lord caused Midian to prevail against Israel because of its sin (6:2). One day the Lord visited Gideon while he was alone in the wine press and greeted Gideon by saying, *"The Lord is with you, O valiant warrior. Go in this your strength and deliver Israel from the hand of Midian"* (v. 12, 14). At first Gideon doubted that it was the Lord addressing him because he was of no rank or power in the land. But after the Lord consumed Gideon's offering with fire, Gideon rose up and at the command of the Lord, he tore down the altar of Baal which belonged to his father (vv. 25-27).

Recognizing the Lord's authority upon him, Gideon then gathered warriors to go against Midian. At the

Lord's command he went up against the camp of Midian and it was subdued before the sons of Israel (Judges 7:9; 8:11, 28). For the next forty years the land was undisturbed. Despite Israel's plea to Gideon for him and his sons to rule over them, he understood the authority received and said to them, *"I will not rule over you, nor shall my son rule over you; the LORD shall rule over you"* (8:22-23). Through Gideon, again we see God establish the authority over a people without the agency of any man of position or rank, and do so with one who was the least of the least in all of his land.

David had a similar experience with the authority he received. After God had rejected Saul from being king over Israel, He told the prophet Samuel to go to the house of Jesse the Bethlehemite, for He had chosen one of Jesse's sons to be king in place of Saul (1 Samuel 16:1). Samuel went as commanded, however, when he saw Jesse's eldest son, Eliab, he thought surely the Lord's anointed stood before him. But the Lord said to the prophet,

> *"Do not look at his appearance or at the height of his stature, because I have rejected him; for God sees not as man sees, for man looks at the outward appearance, but the Lord looks at the heart"* (v. 7).

Jesse then presented six more of his sons to Samuel. None were chosen by the Lord to receive His authority. Then Samuel asked Jesse if there were any more children. That is when David was brought in from tending the sheep and introduced to Samuel. As David approached, the Lord said to Samuel, *"Arise, anoint him; for this is he"*

(v. 12). Then Samuel took his horn of oil and anointed David in the midst of his father and brothers. At that moment the authority of the Lord was vested in David. Although it went unrecognized by his family and his king, it was in that authority that he slayed Goliath and it was in that authority that he served his father, his brothers and King Saul until he himself sat upon the throne of Israel (2 Samuel 5:4).

As with the others to whom the Lord gives His authority, David's calling and authority came without the approval or input of the existing temporal authority structures, even though those authority structures were placed there by God. At all times, God chooses the vessel for His authority by His own will and for His own purpose.

As for David, he like Joseph and Gideon before him understood authority and exercised that authority always aware that at any moment God could revoke it (2 Samuel 15:25-26; 2 Samuel 16:5-11). It is only those who understand authority that exercise authority not as though it were their own but God's, and it is only those who understand authority who do not hold on to authority at all costs.

It was through the lives of these men that the Lord mercifully showed me that His authority rests with and upon, not those who hold titles or rights, but with the instrument of His choosing. In every case, the Lord gives His authority at His will and for His purpose, with no regard given to the existing authority structure, whether be it political, commercial, social, religious, or otherwise. Although at first this revelation was a challenge to the order of things as I understood them, I began to realize that not only was my understanding of the relationship between authority and position misplaced, but my perception of the relationship between authority and order were also not the same as God's; and so I continue to learn Him.

Garments of Skin

While I was writing *The Divine Intention - a Journey to ...Salvation,* I needed to verify the accuracy of something related to Abram. To do so, I needed to read the first eleven chapters of Genesis. As I read, the Lord stopped me at Genesis 3:21. This verse had absolutely nothing to do with what I was trying to verify, but I knew His voice so I paused at the verse. He then said, *"What you think you know about this verse is wrong. The garment of skin is not Me doing what man could not do with the fig leaves. Nor is it a foreshadowing of things to come through the life and death of My Son. The garments of skin are the identifying mark. It identifies the condition of man after their sin. They are death, and death now reigns in them."*

Obviously this flew right in the face of everything I was ever taught about this story, but when He said it, it made perfect sense. The first thing I saw was how the garments of skin could not be a foreshadowing of Jesus or a covering for Adam's sin *"for it is impossible for the blood of bulls and goats to take away sins"* (Hebrews 10:4). The insufficiency of the animal's death in making amends for the sin of Adam is established in the fact that Jesus had to subsequently come and did come. If the garments of skin were representative of the atonement, why then did it not atone? Why then after being covered by the garments did the sin of Adam continue to pass on death and judgment to all men? It would appear that if the garments of skin were representative of Christ and His atonement, given after man's failed attempt to atone himself (with fig leaves), it utterly failed in its representation. Mercifully, since that is not what the garments of skin represent, that is not the case.

The next thing I understood was that the only acceptable sacrifice for sin comes from above not from the earth (John 3:16-17). The garments of skin given by God came from an animal Adam was given dominion over. The animal did not come down from above.

I then saw the truth that Adam was clothed in righteousness from the moment the Lord breathed life into his nostrils. The same was true for Eve after the Lord formed her from the rib of man. They were naked in their flesh, yet not ashamed (Genesis 2:25; Psalm 119:80). (Contrary to the belief of some, Adam and Eve had human flesh from their creation). Their clothing (their righteousness) identified who and what they were. In that identity of righteousness they would have dominion over all of creation and pass that dominion on to their offspring (Genesis 1:26, 28). However, they sinned; acting contrary to their identity, and their clothing was lost. They then stood in their flesh, naked and ashamed. So they clothed themselves in fig leaves because they saw their own nakedness. However, the fig leaves did not identify who or what they had become because of their sin. Unlike the covering of righteousness, the covering of leaves served no identifying purpose and was meaningless. So God made garments of skin (a garment of death) for the man and the woman and clothed them. Their clothing now matched their identity (James 1:15). Now instead of multiplying dominion in the earth, they would multiply death (Genesis 4:8). For by his transgression, Adam passed down to all men judgment, resulting in condemnation (Romans 5:15, 16, 18), and through him many were made sinners and death reigned (5:17, 19). No longer would Adam be identified by righteousness, but by garments of skin.

As alarming and eye-opening as this revelation was, the most frightening part of this experience was to understand the rebellious nature of man; his ability to formulate beliefs, doctrines and faith so completely opposite of truth. I was appalled at myself for ever believing a lie. I began to understand that at every turn, man sees as he wants to see, not as God sees. Man does not want to see himself as death, but as life. Man always sees the world in the best light for himself. Therefore, he chooses to believe accordingly, even if it is completely wrong. I was blind to this reality until the Lord gave me sight. That leads me to the next truth revealed.

I'm Not Saved

This was a most devastating experience. I consider myself very blessed. I do not look with regret at the life that I have been given. Nevertheless, there are some rough days and if there was one thing I could always fall back on regardless of how bad things were or how horrible I felt, it was that I was saved because I had "accepted" Jesus as my Lord and Savior. That was until the Lord told me that I was not saved. That was not one of my better days. It was not that He said I *could not* be saved, but that I *was not* saved.

Before He spoke this, I understood salvation to be everything that you probably understand salvation to be to you as you read this chapter. The fact that I was a new creation and all that was made available to me as a child of God and co-heir with Jesus were well known to me. I lived with an expectation of heaven and I exercised and relied upon the benefits of being a child of the King. But I was wrong and because I was wrong I was in danger of not having that which I thought I had. The reason why was because I thought I already possessed it. Because I thought I possessed it, I no longer sought it out and if I did not seek it out and seek it at the cost of my very life, I would never obtain it (Matthew 10:37-38; 13:46; Luke 9:23; 1 Corinthians 6:19-20; Philippians 2:5-9). Contrary to all that I learned in Christianity about being saved, the Lord was now opening my eyes to two very important things: salvation is not now; and salvation is not free.

The Lord illustrated this reality to me through the account of Him leading the sons of Israel out of Egyptian bondage and to the land promised to Abraham. All of the sons of Israel left Egypt with Moses. All who left also experienced the benefits and protection of the Passover blood and all ate spiritual food and drank spiritual drink. Yet most never made it to the land where God was leading them (1 Corinthians 10:1-5). Most died along the way because they rejected God's commands and His

Lordship.   Most complained and grumbled, always longing for the comforts of Egypt.

The ones who made it to the ultimate destination were the ones who left yesterday behind, gave no thought for tomorrow, and only lived in the now with God, as He led them. They trusted in Him and they trusted Him; with everything. They did not consider the life that they were living to be their own, but His. They moved when He said move; they rested when He said rest. They ate what He gave and were always satisfied in Him. They did this for forty years, until all who did not believe had died. Then they entered into the land flowing with milk and honey and settled there, eating the fruit of the land and conquering it, making the land their own.

By and through the history of this people I saw that salvation did not happen at the exodus from Egypt, but at the crossing of the Jordan at the entrance to the land of promise. I saw that although any and all could leave Egypt, only those who belonged wholly to the Lord, made it through to the Jordan. I saw that those who left Egypt after experiencing the protection of the Passover lamb, but who held on to their life, either physically or emotionally, died with their life in their hand. But those who handed their whole life over to the Lord, without regret, received back their whole life and more, upon entering the land of God's promise.

Finally, I understood that if I am to be saved, it will be salvation from the wrath of God (Romans 5:9-10; 1 Thessalonians 1:10; 5:9; John 3:36) not from the rule of Pharaoh. As the record of the wanderings of the sons of Israel illustrate to us, salvation is not an escape from trials or tribulations or a difficult and unpleasurable life (Luke 4:1-13; 9:58; 2 Corinthians 11:23-27; Isaiah 53:3). Salvation is being delivered from the judgment of God for rebellion and selfish ambition. The sons of Israel experienced this reality. The Lord opened my eyes to see truth and I learned from their experience.

I do have a hope of salvation and that salvation that I hope for I am working out with fear and trembling, not celebration. There is a vast difference. I no longer wake up feeling like I have arrived at the Jordan. Now, I wake up looking to the Lord as He leads me to the Jordan, for even if my name was on the roll as I left Egypt, it may not be on the roll at the Jordan (Revelation 3:5).

Wrestling with God
Is not a Good Idea

Jacob was a man led by his fears. He lived in the terror of his brother's revenge ever since the day he stole Esau's blessing from their father Isaac (Genesis 27:41-45). Twenty years after Jacob's deception, he had grown into a large company of people. He had two wives, eleven children, many servants and much livestock. At that time he sent word to his brother, in the land of Seir asking for his favor (Genesis 32:3-5). Esau replied that he was coming to meet Jacob. It was reported to Jacob that Esau was bringing with him four hundred men. At this news, Jacob became fearful and divided his people into two companies believing that if Esau came and attacked one company, then the other company could escape and he might survive.

Jacob then prayed to the Lord that he be delivered from the hand of his brother. He then prepared an offering of hundreds of animals and sent it with his servants to Esau in the hope of appeasing his brother's wrath. Jacob then sent his wives and children ahead of him and stayed the night alone.

That evening, while alone, a man wrestled with Jacob until daybreak. When the man saw that he had not prevailed against Jacob, he touched the socket of Jacob's thigh so the socket became dislocated. Then the man said, "*Let me go, for the dawn is breaking.*" But Jacob refused to let the man go unless the man first blessed him. The man asked, "*What is your name?*" And he said, "Jacob." The man said, "*Your name shall no longer be Jacob, but Israel; for you have striven with God and with men and have prevailed.*" So the man blessed him there and Jacob named the place Peniel, for he said, "*I have seen God face to face, yet my life has been preserved*" (Genesis 32:24-32).

This account has been interpreted by many Christians to mean that it is proper and even necessary for us to strive with God until He gives a blessing. This understanding is wrong and only furthers the lustful and selfish character of fallen man. Despite God's promise to Jacob to be with him and to bless him in the same way He blessed his grandfather Abraham, Jacob served himself, not God. He was a servant to his own fears and he did not trust the God of his fathers. He contended with man to serve his interests, and he prevailed. Now he contended with God Himself until he received what *he* wanted. He fought with God for a blessing. He did not, like his fathers before him, lay himself down before the Lord in utter surrender and trust. Hosea reveals how God felt about Jacob's actions. There the Lord said He:

"... will punish Jacob according to his ways; He will repay him according to his deeds. In the womb he took his brother by the heel, and in his maturity he contended with God. Yes, he wrestled with the angel and prevailed; he wept and sought His favor" (Hosea 12:2-4).

Jacob's ways of selfish persistence and lack of surrender are still prevalent today. I know because it was in me until the Lord had mercy on me and healed me of my blindness. I was ashamed at how many times I could recall where I banged on the gates of heaven until God answered my prayers. Because my way was cloaked in what is deemed prayer, I was blinded to the lust and fear that drove me. I needed simply to surrender to His love and to His care. I only needed to believe God and trust Him. He was not and is not delighted by my striving with Him for what I want. In the end, He will punish. Until I had eyes to see, I wrestled with God. I wrestle no longer because I desire a name that means Life, not a name that means I contended with God and prevailed (Revelation 2:17; 3:12).

In the Twinkling of an Eye

One day Jesus' disciples asked Him, "What would be the sign of Your coming and the end of the age" (Matthew 24:3)? His reply was remarkably simple and profound.

The first part of the reply was a warning; *"do not be misled"* (Matthew 24:4); *"for many will be misled, even possibly, the elect"* (vv. 11, 23-24, 26, 39; Luke 17:23). The second part of the reply contained commands, *"See that you are not frightened" (v. 6)* and *"Be on the alert...and be ready"* (v. 42, 44, 50; 1 Thessalonians 5:6).

On a different occasion, when speaking of His appearing and the end of the age, He said it is comparable to a man who sowed good seed in his field, but tares sprouted up along with the wheat. So, in the time of the harvest the man will say to the reapers, *"**First gather up the tares** and bind them in bundles to burn them up; but gather the wheat into my barn"* (Matthew 13:24-30). He said it is also comparable to a dragnet that is cast into the sea, gathering fish of every kind. When the net is filled, it is drawn up on the beach. The fishermen then gather the good fish into containers, but the bad fish they threw away. Jesus said,

> *"So it will be at the end of the age; the angels will come forth and **take out the wicked from among the righteous**, and will throw them into the furnace of fire; in that place there will be weeping and gnashing of teeth"* (vv. 49-50).

As to the timing of this gathering up and separation, Jesus said no one knows but the Father (Matthew 24:36), but of that awesome day He said,

> *"The sign of the Son of Man will appear in the sky, and then all the tribes of the earth will mourn, and they will see the Son of Man coming on the clouds of*

the sky with power and great glory. And He will send forth His angels with a great trumpet and they will gather together His elect from the four winds, from one end of the sky to the other" (vv. 30-31).

There is one simple truth to be found in all that Jesus said regarding His return and the end of the age: There are things about which I have control and there are things about which I have no control. What should have been obvious to me was missed. There are only three things that concern me or about which I am responsible. Those are: do not be misled, do not fear; and be ready. Unfortunately, until the Lord opened my eyes, I had spent far too much energy on the things that did not concern me; namely, when and how the Lord would return, what would occur prior to His return, and what He would do when He arrived.

Sadly, I spent years filling my head with the opinions and predictions of man, all of which have proven wrong with time. The longer I live the more I understand that looking for Jesus by watching the world will only lead you to follow the world.

Today, I do not bother with what is going on in the world. I bother with watching and following Jesus. As I do so, I find that it is impossible for me to be misled. To be misled means to be led wrongly. But if I am following Him at all times and in all things, being misled will never happen (John 10:4-5, 27-28). Furthermore, regardless of what comes upon the earth in the form of terrors or persecutions, if I am walking with Jesus there is nothing to fear. The only way for me to fear is to forget about Him and pay more attention to what is happening (Matthew 8:18-27).   So, it is not important that I watch to see what is happening or what may happen.   In all that happens, His response is the same, *"I am yours and you are Mine; only believe."*

And to complete all that for which I am responsible, I need at all times to be ready.   In other words, never let my guard down thinking I can get by for a while without Him.   I must be diligent at all times to follow the Lord and trust in Him only, not looking to the left or to the right.   It only takes an instant to be misled or frightened, and then the trouble really begins (John 18:25-27).

The Least is Greater

The last experience I will share here came to me with great sadness, but an undeniable reality.

The prophet Isaiah referred to him as

"THE VOICE OF ONE CRYING IN THE WILDERNESS, 'MAKE READY THE WAY OF THE LORD, MAKE HIS PATHS STRAIGHT'" (John 1:23)!

John the Baptist was unique among men.   He came baptizing in water so that the Lord might be manifested to Israel (v. 31).   John is the one who declared, *"Behold, the Lamb of God who takes away the sin of the world"* (v. 29)!   It was he, to the exclusion of all others, who heard the Lord speak from heaven saying, *"He upon whom you see the Spirit descending and remaining upon Him, this is the One who baptizes in the Holy Spirit."*   John testified that he saw that which was spoken, and that Jesus is the Son of God (vv. 33-34).

Of him, Jesus said that, *"John himself is Elijah who was to come"* (Matthew 11:14) and *"he is one who is more than a prophet"* (v. 9). And *"Among those born of women there has not arisen anyone greater than John the Baptist! Yet the one who is least in the kingdom of heaven is greater than he"* (v. 11).

With that last statement the Lord opened my eyes to a frightening reality. There is one who is described as least in the kingdom of heaven. Who that may be is not relevant. What is relevant though is what it means to be the least. To be least is to be at the place where there is none below you. There is no one lower than the least. Therefore, if that one is the least in the kingdom of heaven, yet that one is greater than John, then John cannot be in the kingdom of heaven. But how could that be? With all that was spoken of him and with all that he saw and did, how could it be that he would be outside of heaven?

The answer: God is no respecter of man and sin is sin. By his own words, John came baptizing so that Jesus might be manifested to Israel. When Jesus was baptized by John and the Spirit rested upon Him, He was manifested to Israel and John's divine purpose and calling were complete. John himself stated that, Jesus must increase, and he himself must decrease (John 3:30). Yet, this is not what happened. Instead, Scripture records that John continued to baptize *"because there was much water and people were coming"* (v. 23; Acts 19:3-5). Even after Jesus was revealed as the Christ, John still had disciples.

The only right thing to have happened was for John and all of his disciples to stop and follow the One who came after (John 1:35-39). There was no place for two camps. In fact there were three, because in addition to John, the Pharisees had their disciples (Matthew 9:14-17).

This all led to a most tragic end. While in prison, John heard of the works of Jesus and sent some of his disciples to Jesus to question Him saying,

> "Are You the Expected One, or shall we look for someone else?" Jesus answered and said to them, "Go and report to John what you hear and see: the blind receive sight and the lame walk, the lepers are cleansed and the deaf hear, the dead are raised up, and the poor have the gospel preached to them. And blessed is he who does not take offense at Me" (Matthew 11:2-6).

John lost his sight. He lost his way. He lost his faith. He no longer recognized the very Object of his calling. He took offense at God and did not believe. There is no evidence that John ever departed from this position prior to his execution. The reality of this even hit Jesus when news of John's death was reported to Him. He withdrew from where He was to a secluded place by Himself (Matthew 14:13). Jesus was not mourning the fleshly passing of a friend, but the spiritual death of a brother. Knowing what would await John in heaven, there would have been no need for sadness on Jesus' part, for He knew who would be there to welcome him (John 14:28). But there *was* sadness and now we see why.

My Depravity

The common element in all that I have shared is that I was blind to the truth until the Lord gave me sight. That does not mean that I could not see with my natural eyes. I could, only I did not understand or comprehend what I saw, and sadly I was completely unaware of my blindness (Isaiah 6:9-10; John 3:9; Acts 9:1-19).

The Lord found me in depravity, walking blindly about the earth in a set of beliefs that were based upon untruth, and He offered Himself as the Light. I would suggest you reread John 9 at this point.

I heard Him speak; I listened and I believed; I received sight. Each time it was like dying all over again. But it is a death I will repeat as often as He utters His voice (Revelation 2:11; 21:8). You may not yet see what I see, but I pray that you will have eyes to see. I pray that you recognize your condition and your need and not miss your time of visitation. There is much to see.

✦

Chapter 12

REVELATION'S GREATEST ENEMY

(Part II of *Eyes to See*)

Scripture reference:

> *"You have heard that the ancients were told, 'YOU SHALL NOT COMMIT MURDER' and 'Whoever commits murder shall be liable to the court.' But I say to you....*

"You have heard that it was said, 'YOU SHALL NOT COMMIT ADULTERY'; but I say to you....

"It was said, 'WHOEVER SENDS HIS WIFE AWAY, LET HIM GIVE HER A CERTIFICATE OF DIVORCE'; but I say to you...." (Matthew 5:21-22, 27-28, 31-32; see also vv. 33, 38, 43).

In *Eyes to See* I shared with you a few of my experiences with the Lord giving me sight where I was blind. The premise of this chapter being that man cannot see until and unless God gives him sight, much like when Peter called Jesus *"the Christ, the Son of the living God"* because the Father gave him revelation of the truth (Matthew 16:13-17); or like when Paul, after receiving a revelation of the Lord on the road to Damascus, forsook his persecution of the Way and instead began to proclaim Jesus in the synagogues saying, *"He is the Son of God"* (Acts 9:3-6, 20).

All that the Lord revealed to me in those experiences challenged my belief structure, yet it did not shake my faith in Him. Although what He was speaking was contrary to things I had understood to be true, in each instance I chose to release to Him my then-held beliefs and to trust Him and what He was presently revealing. By doing so I found that my relationship to the Lord changed. I also saw things from a completely different perspective, and things that I just assumed to be one way turned out to be the opposite way. Suddenly, the Scriptures made perfect sense. There was no longer a need to assume, stretch, twist, or interpret what He has said (Mark 8:16-17). It was right there before my eyes, like a parable being explained in detail (Mark 4:11-12).

I am thankful to the Lord for all He has shown me, but in this process of gaining sight, I have learned a very disturbing reality. I learned that the greatest danger to revelation is revelation itself. I saw the potential for this danger in my own life as I struggled at times with what the Lord was showing me. You may have experienced this yourself while reading *Eyes to See*. I realized that if there was one thing that could keep me from embracing that which the Lord was now showing me, it would be something that He had shown or spoken previously. I began to recognize the tendency of man to establish a law or canon out of the things that God had spoken, to the exclusion of God Himself. I began to see that what I believed to be a relationship with God was actually a relationship with things He said. My relationship was more with a book or a doctrine than with Him. Despite the difficulty with which these revelations came to me, I was confident that each occasion was an occasion for me to know Him in a way that I did not know Him before.

Blasphemy or Revelation

We see this danger to revelation play out in the lives of the Jewish people in the days of Jesus' earthly ministry.

One Sabbath Jesus was passing by a man who was blind from birth (John 9:1, 14). His disciples asked Him whether it was the man's sin or the sin of his parents that caused him to be born in such a condition. Jesus responded that it was neither. He explained that the man was born blind *"so that the works of God might be displayed in him"* (v. 3). The Lord then declared, *"I am the Light of the world"* (v. 5). He then healed the man of his blindness.

After questioning the man about how he received his sight, the Pharisees concluded that the One who healed him was not from God *"because He did not keep the Sabbath"* (v. 16). They later declared Him to be a sinner (v. 24). In justifying their position in the matter, the Pharisees said to the man, *"You are His disciple, but we are disciples of Moses. We know that God has spoken to Moses, but as for this man, we do not know where He is from"* (vv. 28-29).

Through His encounter with this young man the Lord was showing to all men the human condition and the human need. The condition is blindness and the need is Light. And to that condition and need Jesus declared that He is the Light (vv. 35-38). *This* was the work of God being displayed in the man. However, *this* work went unrecognized by the people because of a previous revelation they had received from God; the Sabbath law.

Until the Lord spoke to Moses concerning the Sabbath, it did not exist (Exodus 16:22-30). It had zero meaning or purpose to Israel. However, by the time Jesus healed the young man on this particular Sabbath, Israel had taken what God said to Moses and made it canonical. To make something canonical is to establish something as perpetually accepted, approved, official, and undisputed.[1] It is upon this that religion establishes faith. According to the Pharisees, the Sabbath had official and undisputable standards of conduct and Jesus violated those standards;

therefore, He could not be from God. So what prevented the people from seeing the truth of their condition and their true need as God was then speaking was their reliance upon something God had previously spoken.

This danger can affect even the closest of the Lord's disciples. Few were as close to Jesus as Peter, yet after all of his experiences with the Lord, even through Pentecost, Peter struggled with obeying the Lord in the face of violating the Laws of Moses. This occurred when God instructed Peter to go to the house of Cornelius, a gentile who feared God and prayed to Him continually (Acts 10:1-2, 5, 19-20). Prior to being summoned to go to Cornelius, Peter fell into a trance and *saw*

"the sky opened up, and an object like a great sheet coming down, lowered by four corners to the ground, and there were in it all kinds of four-footed animals and crawling creatures of the earth and birds of the air. A voice came to him, 'Get up, Peter, kill and eat!' But Peter said, 'By no means, Lord, for I have never eaten anything unholy and unclean.' Again a voice came to him a second time, 'What God has cleansed, no longer consider unholy'" (vv. 11-15).

Three times Peter saw this vision and three times he refused to kill and eat. However, when the servants of Cornelius came for Peter, he went with them without misgivings because he knew it was the Lord (v. 20). When Peter arrived at Cornelius' house in Caesarea he said to them,

"You yourselves know how unlawful it is for a man who is a Jew to associate with a foreigner or to visit him; and yet God has shown me that I should not call any man unholy or unclean. That is why I came without even raising any objection when I was sent for" (vv. 28-29).

Peter then began to share the good news of the Gospel of Jesus (vv. 36-43). To Peter's amazement, while he was still proclaiming to the house of Cornelius that Jesus is the Christ, the Holy Spirit fell upon all those who were listening and they began speaking with tongues and exalting God. Peter then baptized them in the name of Jesus Christ (vv. 44-48).

As a result, Cornelius and his entire house were born into the kingdom of God. This would have never occurred had Peter held on to the revelation that he possessed concerning not eating anything unclean, which revelation he received from God, through Moses (Leviticus 11; Deuteronomy 14). Like the Pharisees before him, the potential for lost revelation was there for Peter, but because he surrendered his beliefs to the Lord, whom he knew, the Lord was able to reveal to Peter something greater about Himself than Peter understood; *"that God is not one to show partiality, but in every nation the man who fears Him and does what is right is welcome to Him" (vv. 34-35).*

History is full of examples of men struggling with something God says because of something God has said (Mark 7:14-23). Can you relate to Abraham when God commanded him to sacrifice Isaac <u>after</u> God promised him not only a son in his advanced age, but a line of descendants that would number as the stars of heaven (Genesis 15:4-5; 22:2)? You may have glossed over that in your reading of that story, but that *is* the test given to Abraham by God. Will he trust in what God said, or will he trust in what God is saying? Will he worship the word spoken, or will he worship the Speaker?

Or can you see the conflict nearly 2,000 years later with James and the other apostles and elders of the Church as they struggled with the revelation of salvation through faith (Romans 3:21-22; Ephesians 2:8)? The reality of this struggle is evidenced during Paul's visit to the elders in Jerusalem and in his words to the churches (Acts 15:4-5; Romans 1:15-17; 2:28-29; 3:18; Galatians 2:16; Ephesians 2:11-22; Philippians 3:1-11; Colossians 2:11). To the Jewish brethren, this message of salvation seemed to nullify the Law, as it rendered irrelevant a circumcision of the flesh as prescribed by the Law of Moses (Acts 15:1, 6-7). Paul, however, pointed out that it in no way nullified the Law, but to the contrary, established the Law in that

"The Scripture, foreseeing that God would justify the Gentiles by faith, preached the gospel beforehand to Abraham, saying, "All the nations will be blessed in you." So then those who are of faith are blessed with Abraham, the believer" (Galatians 3:8-9).

In the instances of Abraham and James, as with Peter in Caesarea, they chose to trust the Speaker rather than the spoken (Genesis 22:11-12; Acts 15:19, 28), but Paul's continuing battle within the churches would suggest that not all made that same choice.

What blinded those who continued to rely upon the words spoken at the expense of listening to the Speaker, was a hardened heart. Because of their hardness of heart they suppressed the truth in unrighteousness. *"They became futile in their speculations"* and their hearts were darkened. *"Professing to be wise, they became fools"* (Romans 1:21-22) as in the case of the Pharisees when they accused Jesus and His disciples of breaking the Sabbath by picking and eating the heads of grain as they walked through the grain fields (Matthew 12:1-2). Jesus rebuked them saying,

> *"Have you not read in the Law, that on the Sabbath the priests in the temple break the Sabbath and are innocent? But I say to you that something greater than the temple is here. But if you had known what this means, 'I desire compassion, and not a sacrifice,' you would not have condemned the innocent"* (vv. 5-7).

Is He dead or alive?

The problem is not God's word. The problem is what man does with God's word. When God speaks His word it is Life, relevant and applicable to the moment for those to whom it is spoken. But when men take that word, limit it to its original meaning and intent, and make it apply to other men at other times in other situations apart from God speaking at that time, they establish an environment for rebellion against God. They have now created a relationship with a law instead of with the Lawgiver and are unwilling to depart from the law, even if it is God Himself who speaks concerning the law.

God is a "now" God (Matthew 6:25-34; Luke 12:35-40; Hebrews 3:13; 4:7; James 4:14; Revelation 3:20). He lives in absolute time and operates in the immediate present. He does so by speaking and leading. However, by relying only on what God has said and not on what He is saying, men have made Him into a "then" God (Matthew 19:1-9; John 8:5; 9:29; Luke 13; 14). This is one of the problems with making canonical something that God has said. It eliminates the need for a continuing relationship with God, the Speaker of the word. It keeps God in the past as if He were dead. Because canon codifies what God has said, man is no longer dependent on God for anything more as it concerns that word that was spoken. In practice, it is no longer God who is obeyed and worshipped, but the canon. In the case of the Sabbath law; it is not that the Sabbath law was not God's word when He spoke it to Moses; it was and it was to be obeyed. The issue is that man took ownership of that law and canonized God right out of His own word (Matthew 12:8-14). This is exactly what Jesus encountered in the Pharisees when He gave sight to the blind man (John 9:16).

At the outset of the Lord's opening my eyes, He showed me that He wants me to live by every word that proceeds forth from His mouth (Isaiah 55:1-3; Matthew 4:4). He did not want me living by what He *said*, but by what He *says*. I then realized that I had made the same mistake so many before me had made. The walking out of my faith relied upon the words spoken at the expense of listening to the Speaker. I may have declared that I loved and served a living God, but my actions proved without a doubt that God was dead and He left a record of His statements behind for me to follow. I was living according to what He said, not what He was saying. I realized that had I been present on the day that Jesus gave sight to the blind man I too would have accused Him of being a sinner.

He told me to walk with Him and that His word would proceed forth as a daily event (Matthew 6:11), not unlike the daily manna given to the sons of Israel as they left Egypt. I knew as never before that I had made the Bible my God.

As I mentioned earlier, I learned a very disturbing reality in these times of gaining sight. I learned that my blindness was my doing. The truth of God is evident within me, because God made it so, but in unrighteousness I suppressed the truth. I have since repented and now I see and I am free; free to proclaim to you a freedom that is yours in Christ Jesus; a freedom to live with, walk with, hear, love, and obey a living God. Do not let fear stop you.

✦

Chapter 13

The Taskmaster

We have found the Messiah!

As a result of this many of His disciples withdrew and were not walking with Him anymore. So Jesus said to the twelve, "You do not want to go away also, do you?" Simon Peter answered Him, "Lord, to whom shall we go? You have words of eternal life. We have believed and have come to know that You are the Holy One of God" (John 6:66-69).

Truly, truly, I say to you, when you were younger, you used to gird yourself and walk wherever you wished; but when you grow old, you will stretch out your hands and someone else will gird you, and bring you where you do not wish to go." Now this He said, signifying by what kind of death he would glorify God. And when He had spoken this, He said to him, "Follow Me" (John 21:18-19)!

There is always that initial excitement and exhilaration upon hearing the news that the Christ is come. Take for instance the accounts of Andrew and Nathanael. Andrew was a disciple of John the Baptist. One day as Jesus walked near, John said to his disciple, *"Behold, the Lamb of God"* (John 1:36)! Immediately, Andrew and another of John's disciples followed Jesus. After spending the day with Him, Andrew told his brother Simon that he had *"found the Messiah"* (v. 41).

The next day Jesus found Philip and said to him, *"Follow Me"* (v. 43). Philip in turn found Nathanael and said to him, *"We have found Him of whom Moses in the*

Law and also the Prophets wrote" (v. 45). After hearing from Jesus for himself, Nathanael declared, *"You are the Son of God; You are the King of Israel"* (v. 49).

When you first encounter the Lord Jesus there is a fondness, previously unknown. His unconditional love is convicting and His forgiveness is uplifting and liberating. Whatever troubled the heart prior to the Divine encounter is extinguished and replaced with a peace and a joy that is not from this world. The experience is uniquely human and extraordinary. But then as a matter of necessity everything changes. It changes because maturity is in sight. Regardless of the station in life or the circumstances that led to the Divine encounter, the Heavenly aim is to move toward fullness. On this path to fullness Jesus becomes uncomfortably unfamiliar (Luke 18:18-26; John 4:27, 31-34). The Jesus you met at the first is nowhere to be found and you feel strangely alone. You search for your Friend only to discover that He has walked on ahead, simply saying, "Follow Me." If obedience is the response to His command, ultimately maturity is reached along with the knowledge that He is the Holy One of God (see Galatians 4:19; Ephesians 4:13). If His command is met with reluctance, regret, or doubt, the sight of Him fades as He continues on His path (Mark 10:21-22; Luke 7:19).

What Did You Say?

I was raised in a Catholic family. My familiarity with God was by way of the church, its functions, and its priesthood. During my childhood I was content in that arrangement. It was what I knew. As I progressed through my teenage years I sought a deeper understanding about life, death, and eternity. I was very familiar with the historical Jesus, as He was spoken about often during the Catholic mass and catechism. Nevertheless, what I knew was not satisfying my need. I asked questions and got no answers. I was empty to say the least, but I kept on searching. This continued into my early twenties.

Then one evening the Lord came near. He met me in my room as I lay upon my bed. He physically touched me. I did not see Him with my eyes, but I felt Him throughout my body. It was like being electrocuted while at the same time being crushed by a 2-ton boulder. The reality floored me. Actually, it terrified me. Within seconds of His touch, I begged Him to stop. He did. Then He was gone. I was filled with both dread and excitement. I felt His holiness and I knew my sinfulness. After a few moments passed I regretted asking Him to leave, but one thing was for sure, He was there; He was real! For years I had heard about Him with my ears, but now I had met Him. There was no doubt, I would now follow Him. And follow Him I did.

Suddenly, I had understanding. Days, weeks, and months went by and it seemed as if everything made sense. The years of emptiness were gone. I just wanted to know Him. I seemed to have direction and purpose in life. I began to read books and listen to people who professed an encounter with Him. I was able to relate to everything I heard and read. It was so different than what I had known before. I just could not get enough.

Then, abruptly, there was nothing. It stopped. I was no longer hearing and I understood even less. Even though I was still seeking after Him as I had done for months, I could not find Him and I did not know why.

I asked those who professed knowledge of Him and the only answer I received was that I must be in sin. They said, "Something was hindering [my] continued fellowship with God; otherwise [I] would not be experiencing this silence." Since I figured they knew God better than I did, I was okay with that explanation. The only problem was I was completely unaware of any sin. So now I was lost and no one could explain to me where I was.

After this time of silence that seemed like months, but was more like several weeks, I began hearing again. However, the things I was now hearing were different from what I had heard in the months since I met Him in my room. I was hearing strange things; crazy things. Not crazy as in "science fiction crazy" but crazy as in this makes no sense crazy.

At that time in my life, I had recently graduated from college and began dating the girl who would be my wife. Life was great. I was set to begin my career in business with my father. I grew up watching him in his work. I knew it. I understood it. I liked it. I was ready to join him in it and work toward building a family – it was my dream. But I was hearing the Lord tell me to go in another direction professionally. He was instructing me to prepare to take the law school entrance exam. He wanted me to become a lawyer.

Unexpectedly, our relationship changed. What began as excitement and exhilaration turned into indifference as I struggled with the disappointment to and the derailment of my life plan. What He was saying to me now was the absolute last thing in the world I wanted to hear. I thought, "More school; are you kidding me? I just finished sixteen years of school." I said, "God, I do not want nor do I need more school. And if I go back to school, I cannot begin a family. What I had planned for my life could be done with the education I now have. Oh, and by the way, I do not even like attorneys."

I grappled with what was happening and why it was happening? I thought the goal was achieved when I met Him and followed Him. I did not expect to encounter any personal challenge. This is not what I understood a relationship with Jesus to be.

Then the Lord made me to understand that I was no longer my own. I belonged to Him. I was reminded that during the years of seeking Him that led me to this very moment, that I had surrendered my life to Him. In my repeated profession of faith, I had voluntarily made Him my master and Lord. I was *now* His possession and His bond-servant. I was not now free to choose my path, as I had yielded my will to His. For the first time, I was seeing my profession of faith become a reality.

Even though it was unfamiliar, unexpected, and initially discouraging, it was Him and it was His will. The relationship was then understood; Jesus went from being a wonderful Messiah to a wonderful Teacher and Lord. He became my Taskmaster, and it was He who I had to follow; I must.

The Necessity of Agreement

Jesus came revealing the Father (John 14:7). He came preaching and teaching the kingdom of heaven (Matthew 13; Luke 4:43). In doing so, He frequently likened the kingdom of heaven to a master-servant relationship. Take for example that relationship as it is described in Matthew 24:45 through the *"faithful and sensible slave whom his master put in charge of his household,"* or the Master-servant relationship described in Matthew 25:14-30 through the man who, before leaving on a journey, *"called his own slaves and entrusted his possessions to them."* (See also Mark 13:33-36; John 13:13-16; Luke 12:35-48; Luke 16:1-9).

Jesus made it very clear that the kingdom of God is a kingdom that functions in the context of a Master/slave relationship. It is evident through a reading of each of those parables that unless one falls in line with the reality of that kingdom relationship by way of complete and total submission to the Master, that there will be grave consequences. We must come to the place where we understand that to live in the kingdom of heaven requires agreement with the reality of heaven. That is why the question is asked, *"Can two walk together unless they are in agreement"* (see Amos 3:3; John 17:21-23)? One may follow after Another, but for the two to walk together, there must be agreement.

Many walked after Jesus. But few walked together with Him. The Gospel of John illustrates this truth clearly. There it is recorded that Jesus fed nearly five thousand one day as He ministered to them near the Sea of Galilee.

The next day He left for Capernaum. Those who were fed the day before followed after Jesus. When they found Him He said to them, *"Truly, truly, I say to you, you seek Me, not because you saw signs, but because you ate of the loaves and were filled. Do not work for the food which perishes, but for the food which endures to eternal life, which the Son of Man will give to you, for on Him the Father, God, has set His seal"* (6:26-27). Jesus then proceeded to feed them the food which endures by saying to them, *"I am the living bread that came down out of heaven; if anyone eats of this bread, he will live forever; and the bread also which I will give for the life of the world is My flesh"* (v. 51). Jesus continued on, saying, *"Unless you eat the flesh of the Son of Man and drink His blood, you have no life in yourselves. He who eats My flesh and drinks My blood has eternal life, and I will raise him up on the last day. For My flesh is true food, and My blood is true drink. He who eats My flesh and drinks My blood abides in Me, and I in him"* (vv. 53-56). As a result of these words, even those called His disciples withdrew and were not walking with Him anymore (v. 66).

If this were not enough look what those *"who believed Him"* did after He told them that He is *"the Light of the world and that the one who follows Him will not walk in the darkness, but will have the Light of life"* (John 8:12, 31-32, 59). Where there was no agreement, there was no togetherness. Nothing has changed. The same holds true today.

Most followers of Jesus are familiar with the likes of: Joseph, son of Jacob; Moses; Noah; Samuel; Jeremiah; Elijah; Ezekiel; Jonah; Daniel; Hosea; Esther; Abraham;

Mary, mother of Jesus; Stephen; and Paul. What did each of these have in common? The answer is they did not just follow after the Lord, they each came into agreement with Him; they each walked together with Him - He the Master, they the servant. Their lives were lost in Him and in Him they found Life. They knew Him, not simply as "the Messiah" but as Lord; as Taskmaster.

Whatever it was that He commanded, they did, even at the risk of their life. (Luke 9:24; John 14:15). Moses returned to Pharaoh at the risk of death. (Exodus 3:10). Mary said, "*May it be done to me according to your word.*" (Luke 1:38). Esther said, "*I will go in to the king, which is not according to the law; and if I perish, I perish.*" (Esther 4:16). Hosea was commanded to take a wife of harlotry and have children of harlotry. (Hosea 1:2). Jeremiah was commanded to pronounce judgements against his king and his people, and then told he would neither, take a wife, nor have children. (Jeremiah 1:9-10, 16-17; 16:2). Finally, Paul was shown how much he must suffer for the Lord's name's sake (Acts 9:16). These saints knew and were known by this Master-servant relationship (Genesis 18:3; Exodus 4:10; Daniel 6:20; Ephesians 3:1; Philippians 1:1; 2 Peter 1:1; Jude 1:1), and this Master-servant relationship is how *all* who are His know Him and how all who are His are known by Him. (John 10:4-5; Revelation 14:4).

Contemporary Christianity at best preaches a message of "follow after the Lord and you will be fed." We see this so plainly by the continuous flocking to the blessings and miracles. Regardless of the medium, people are running to and fro just to be filled. Television, radio, and arenas are filled with crowds following after Jesus to be fed again.

To lose one's life so as to find Life at the hands of the Taskmaster is a message that is practically unknown, or mostly rejected. (Luke 9:24). The message is rejected because of a love for self. (John 3:19). The overall rejection of this kingdom message (surrender to the Master) is also seen in one of Christianity's favorite lines, "Come as you are!" The invitation is fine, *only* if you understand that from that point on you *cannot* remain as you are. However, a simple examination of practical Christian ministry establishes that this requirement for change is never the demand made upon its adherents.

He Never Changes and
He Never Stays the Same

God never changes and what never changes about Him is that He will always change. This truth is two-fold. In the first sense, man has the erroneous idea that God is this stagnant being who remains immovable like some 500-ton stone statue. God never changes, yes! His faithfulness is shown to all generations (Psalm 100:5). He will forever be faithful to His Word and to Himself (Deuteronomy 7:9). His lovingkindness is new every morning. His mercy is given freely to all men. (Psalm 136; 145:8-9) *And* at every "opportunity" He will repent of His judgment (2 Chronicles 7:13-14; Jeremiah 26:3; Malachi 3:8-12; Romans 6:23). That does not mean that the "opportunity" is always there, but when it is, He takes it. Each and every time a man repents of his sin God will repent of His judgment against that man. (Ezekiel 18:21-29). God's repeated mercy upon the sons of Israel as recorded in the Book of Judges is but one example of this. Thank God for His never-changing changeableness!

In the other sense, the Lord will only allow a man to remain in a place with Him long enough to see. (Luke 24:13-31). Then He will change; He will move on; He will become unfamiliar. If one is to come to know what he has seen in Jesus, he must follow after Him and he must come into agreement with the Lord and what He has spoken or revealed. Otherwise that man will lose what Light he was shown and he will remain blind (John 9).

The night the Lord visited me in my room, I learned something of Him that I knew not. But that knowledge was but a single step along a Divine path to perfection. (Matthew 5:48; James 1:2). The same is true for the day He commanded that I prepare for law school instead of a career in insurance and it has been the same every day since for over 25 years now. Time and time again, the Lord has shown Himself to me. He has spoken His Will and He has walked on. When He walked, He walked, silently as He awaited my obedience. Then He spoke again. Every time He speaks it is challenging to me, but He desires nonetheless that I accept the challenge and follow after Him, not weighing the cost or having regret, but following after the One that I love. (Luke 14:16-24).

If Jesus has never become strange to you, then question whether you are walking with Him or whether you have stopped and are camped around an image of Him. If the Jesus you know today is the same Jesus you met years ago, then it is likely you are in relationship with a photograph of Jesus; one that you recall with fondness; one that you want to hold on to; one that you show to everybody. The living Jesus likes to walk and He walks as a Taskmaster. You will not need to show anyone the living Jesus, as you do a photograph. He will be seen. (Matthew 5:16).

Chapter 14

The Message of the Kingdom:

Sinlessness

Heaven's Appeal

After forming man out of the dust of the ground and breathing life into him, the Lord put man into the garden that He planted toward the east, in Eden to cultivate it and keep it. The Lord then commanded the man, saying,

> "*From any tree of the garden you may eat freely; but from the tree of the knowledge of good and evil you shall not eat, for in the day that you eat from it you will surely die*" (Genesis 2:7-8, 15-17).

In time, the man disregarded the command of the Lord and ate from the forbidden tree. The Lord then said to the man,

> "Because you have...eaten from the tree about which I commanded you, saying, 'You shall not eat from it'; cursed is the ground because of you; in toil you will eat of it all the days of your life. Both thorns and thistles it shall grow for you; and you will eat the plants of the field; by the sweat of your face you will eat bread, till you return to the ground, because from it you were taken; for you are dust, and to dust you shall return" (Genesis 3:17-19).

The Lord then removed the man from the garden and returned him to the place from which he was taken. (v. 23).

When Cain became angry after the Lord took pleasure in his brother Able and in his brother's offering but had no regard for Cain or for his offering, the Lord said to Cain,

> "Why are you angry? And why has your countenance fallen? If you do well, will not your countenance be lifted up? And if you do not do well, sin is crouching at the door; and its desire is for you, but you must master it" (Genesis 4:6-7).

In time, as Cain and his brother were alone in the field, Cain murdered his brother Able. (v. 8).

⁂

In the tenth generation from Adam the Lord saw that earth was corrupt and filled with violence and that the intent of the thoughts of man's heart was evil and He regretted making man. (Genesis 6:5-7, 11). In the midst of this corruption and violence there lived a righteous man, a man who walked with God and *"a man who did according to all that the Lord had commanded him"* (Genesis 6:9, 22). His name was Noah. God said to Noah, *"I am about to destroy the earth and all flesh...[so]...make for yourself an ark...and this is how you shall make it"* (vv. 13-15).

For eighty years Noah constructed an ark just as the Lord commanded (v.22). He did so in the face of the ridicule and persecution from the men around him. He obeyed the Lord despite the apparent inaction on the part of God and he did it without sin.[1] The Lord preserved Noah along with his family, when He brought a flood upon the world of the ungodly. (Genesis 6:9; 7:1; 2 Peter 2:5).

⁂

1. There is no record that God spoke with Noah between the words recorded in Genesis 6:13-22 and those recorded in Genesis 7:1-5. That would mean that Noah lived by faith in what God spoke in Genesis 6 and did so despite God's silence for nearly 80 years. (Genesis 5:32; 7:6; Hebrews 11:7).

When Abram was seventy-five years old God commanded him to leave his father's house and go forth to a land that the Lord would show him, and there the Lord would bless him and make him a great nation. (Genesis 12:1-4). Abram obeyed, *"and he went out, not knowing where he was going"* (Hebrews 11:8). When Abram was ninety-nine years old, again the Lord appeared to Abram and said to him,

> *"I am God Almighty; Walk before Me, and be blameless. I will establish My covenant between Me and you, and I will multiply you exceedingly.... No longer shall your name be called Abram, but your name shall be Abraham; for I have made you the father of a multitude of nations"* (Genesis 17:1-2, 5).

God fulfilled His promise to Abraham as evidenced by Paul's words to the Galatians when he said, *"if you belong to Christ, then you are Abraham's descendants, heirs according to promise"* (Galatians 3:29).

Even after the sons of Israel rejected the Lord as their king, and God gave them the desire of their heart - a king like the nations around them, He said to them through the prophet Samuel,

> *"If you will fear the LORD and serve Him, and listen to His voice and not rebel against the command of the LORD, then both you and also the king who reigns over you will follow the LORD your God. If you will*

not listen to the voice of the L*ORD*, but rebel against the command of the L*ORD*, then the hand of the L*ORD* will be against you, as it was against your fathers" (1 Samuel 12:14-15).

<hr />

After Solomon had finished building the Temple, the L*ORD* appeared to Solomon and said to him,

"If you will walk before Me....doing according to all that I have commanded you and will keep My statutes and My ordinances, then I will establish the throne of your kingdom over Israel forever.... But if you...turn away from following Me, and do not keep My commandments and My statutes which I have set before you...then I will cut off Israel from the land which I have given them, and the house which I have consecrated for My name, I will cast out of My sight" (1 Kings 9:1-2, 4-7).

<hr />

To all the cities of Judah in the beginning of the reign of Jehoiakim the son of Josiah, king of Judah, the Lord said,

"If you will not listen to Me, to walk in My law which I have set before you, to listen to the words of My servants the prophets, whom I have been sending to you again and again, but you have not listened; then I will make this house like Shiloh, and this city I will

make a curse to all the nations of the earth" (Jeremiah 26:1-6).

As evidenced by the destruction of Jerusalem and the Temple at the hands of Nebuchadnezzar, the sons of Israel and their kings failed to listen to and heed the words of the Lord.

From the moment that God breathed life into man, He has commanded that man live a life free of sin. Even before man ever disobeyed the word of the Lord, God said that life would flow out of man's obedience and warned man that his sin would result in death (Genesis 2:16-17; Romans 6:23). So why then has man continually ignored Heaven's appeal? Why is sin so rampant in humanity?

Sin! What Sin?

The primary reason sin is widespread in the earth is because sin is first a spiritual matter. (Romans 3:23; 5:12-14). Since most men are carnal and not spiritual they are unable to see or understand sin. (1 Corinthians 1:18; 2:14; 2 Corinthians 4:3-4). Take for example the inhabitants of the earth in the days of Noah. Though he preached righteousness for nearly 100 years, none came to recognize their sinfulness. (2 Peter 2:5a). What about the sons of Israel as they were led by God through the wilderness? Though Moses continually rebuked their sinfulness, they thought themselves to be holy. (Numbers

15:32-16:3).   Finally, consider also the people of Jerusalem in the days of Jesus' ministry. He called them to repentance and they did not answer (Luke 19:41-44). In each of these cases we see carnal man unable to recognize a spiritual matter.

Sin is first a spiritual matter because it addresses man's relationship to God. (1 John 3:6). God is spirit, not flesh, even though Jesus took the form of flesh so as to bring salvation to man. (John 4:24; Philippians 2:6-7). Men therefore must relate to God in spirit. (John 4:24). When man relates to God in such manner he lives as a spiritual man and he becomes aware of his fallen condition and repents of his sin. (Luke 5:1-11; 19:1-10). If man does not relate to God in spirit, such man lives as a carnal man and is dead in his sin because he remains unaware of his sinfulness. (John 3:4-8).

In drawing a distinction between the carnal man and the spiritual man, it should be pointed out that when referring to the spiritual man, reference is made not to one who has religion or spirituality (earthly), rather reference is made only to one who is born of the Spirit of God and lives by the word of God (heavenly) (John 3:6; Deuteronomy 8:3; Isaiah 55:2-3). When referring to the carnal man, reference is made both to the one who commits carnal acts or who lives without any reference to God (1 Corinthians 5:1; Ephesians 2:12), and to the one who, although demonstrating an outward recognition of God, has carnal thinking; thinking with the mind of man rather than the mind of God. (1 Corinthians 3:1-3).

A man may be a very good man; not committing "sinful" acts associated with carnality, but is thinking carnally nonetheless. Nicodemus is the primary example of this carnal man. He was the teacher of Israel. Presumably he lived an outwardly sanctified life, yet he could not understand with his carnal mind how it was possible that a man could be born again. (John 3:4-10). The spiritual man has the mind of Christ and operates by faith upon the wisdom of God via the Spirit. The carnal man operates by the wisdom of man via the intellect and finds no value in the words of God. (Hebrews 11).

In other words, the carnal man does not consider his conduct as being sinful. Therefore, to speak to him of living a life free of sin is an insult to his moral independence (Proverbs 16:2; 21:2), or an insult to the freedom he has in Christ Jesus, whichever the case may be. (Galatians 5:13-24; 1 Peter 2:16). In the end, the carnal man, whether carnal in action or carnal in thought, is not seeking to live without sin. (Matthew 6:33).

That is Not Possible!

When I say to a typical Christian that we, as disciples of Jesus, should seek to live a sinless life, I am always met with two responses:

(1) "That is impossible because we are not perfect and God does not expect us to be, that is why He sent Jesus to die for us"; and

(2) "So, are you saying you do not sin?"

Regardless how many times I hear them, the responses are astounding in light of the message of the kingdom.

(Matthew 3:2; 4:17; Mark 1:15; 6:12; Luke 13:3). My reply to the responses is always the same:

(1) "It is not only possible, it is demanded"; and

(2) "Yes, I can and do live free of sin."

If living a sinless life were impossible, Jesus would never have commanded anyone to *"go, and sin no more"* (John 8:11; John 5:14) nor would He have said, when teaching on personal conduct, *"you are to be perfect, as your Father in heaven is perfect"* (Matthew 5:48). Without God, yes, it is impossible to live a life without sin. However, once we are redeemed by God and forgiven of our sin through the cross of Christ, we then have the power of God within us to choose not to sin. With God, a sinless life is the standard. (2 Peter 3:14; 1 John 3:6). This is the message that the Apostle John brought to the church when he wrote,

> *"If we say that we have no sin, we are deceiving ourselves and the truth is not in us. If we confess our sins, He is faithful and righteous to forgive us our sins and to cleanse us from all unrighteousness. If we say that we have not sinned, we make Him a liar and His word is not in us"* (1 John 1:8-10).

The Apostle was simply confirming the words of Paul when he wrote to the church in Rome that the whole world is accountable to God, *because by the works of the Law no flesh is justified in His sight,...for all have sinned and fall short of the glory of God"* (Romans 3:19-20; 23).

However, "*if I have been crucified with Christ, it is no longer I who live, but Christ lives in me*" (Galatians 2:20) and the One who lives in me cannot sin. (Hebrews 4:15). Therefore, "*no one who is born of God practices sin, because His seed abides in him; and he cannot sin*" (1 John 3:9). A sinless life is the life that God lives in me more than the life that I live in Him. (John 5:19; 14:19-21, 23; 15:4). When He lives in me, then I live a sinless life, because He cannot sin. It is He, not I that does not sin.

On the other hand, if I do not live a sinless life, then Christ does not live in me because He does not sin. He may be next to me. He may come near to me. He may feed me and teach me and heal me. But He does not live in me, and only He living in me is Life eternal. Eternal life is not food, knowledge, or miracles. Just ask Adam, Cain, the people of earth in Noah's day, the sons of Israel, and the people who lived in the time of Jesus' earthly ministry who ate the bread He gave and heard the teachings He spoke and received the healings and deliverances He performed. Yet, none knew Him and none had eternal life because sinlessness was not a part of them.

The End of all Things

The message of the kingdom is the message that is proclaimed from heaven. It is the seed sown from above into the earth. (Matthew 3:2; Mark 4:14). It has been declared by the servants of the Most High throughout the history of man. The message ushers in the Divine Intention, which has been from the beginning and is the reason for which all things take place to the glory of Him who accomplishes His will. (Ephesians 1:4).

In each generation of human history, the message is either accepted or rejected. What can be said of those who accepted the message is that they had the end in view. They believed God and they trusted Him. By faith, they saw the harvest that was to come forth from the seed sown. Seeing the harvest from the outset, they found the purpose in the message, and knowing the purpose they gained understanding and appreciation for that which was proclaimed. The harvest of the message is mankind's fellowship with God. It is his unbroken, uninterrupted, and uninhibited communion with the Creator and Father of all.

Though thoroughly spiritual in nature the harvest of the message is given a physical dimension, if for no other reason than to relate the message of the kingdom to mankind. Those who see this physical dimension spiritually find the message and its purpose. (John 4:24; Philippians 2:6-8). As a result they respond to the call and the Lord reaps from that which He has sown. On the other hand, those who fail to see the physical dimension spiritually are ever-consumed with speculations about the physical dimension and are never able to give attention to the message or its purpose.

This physical dimension is called the holy city, New Jerusalem. It is described to creation in some detail as to its walls, gates, streets, and foundational stones. (Revelation 21:12-21). Its light is given by the Lord Himself and in the city there is neither pain nor mourning. (v.v. 4, 23). Again, because few see the physical dimension of the message spiritually, much has been made of these physical details and most are looking to their literal manifestation. However, the most important detail and the one that is rarely addressed in preaching and teaching is that detail which describes the inhabitants of the holy city. The city is inhabited by those who overcome and whose names are written in the Lamb's book of life. (v.v. 7, 27) Moreover, *"nothing unclean, and no one who practices abomination and lying, shall ever come into it"* (v.v. 8, 27).

Those who have eyes to see, see and understand that despite its obvious splendor, with its precious stones and pure gold, the defining characteristic of this city is that it is without darkness, without sin, and without death. The one who is counted among its inhabitants is the one in who there is found no darkness, no sin. In fact, the darkness and the sin are separated out and cast away, having no part in the holy city. (Matthew 13:47-50).

Those who have had this end in view have heeded the message of the kingdom, understanding the purpose and intent of the proclamation to live a life of sinlessness. Today we hear the message – live life without sin. Will we be among those who gain understanding and act on its wisdom? If so, we will be among the few.

Chapter 15

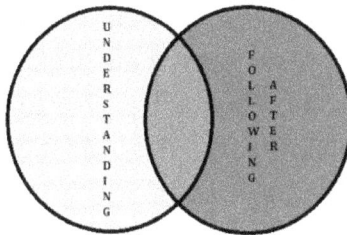

Where Understanding and

Following After Unite

"Sell... Give... and Come, Follow Me!"

With these words the Lord invited a young man to enter into eternal life. Upon hearing them, the young man became sad and went away grieving. (Mark 10:21-22). The Lord then turned to His disciples and said, *"How hard it will be for those who are wealthy to enter the kingdom of God"* (v. 23)!

I must confess that over the years I too easily criticized this man and his appointment with the Lord.[1] His encounter with the Lord was not as spontaneous as it may appear and his response to the Lord not as simple as I supposed. To begin with, I underestimated his sincerity and his effort to obtain eternal life. This should have been gleaned from his life-long adherence to God's law which brought no negative response from the Lord, and from the humility he displayed before the Lord. This humility is seen in two ways. First, he, being a ruler in some measure, came and bowed down on his knees before Jesus. Second, and more meaningful, is that he respected and accepted the Lord's answer to his question. If he did not respect the Lord or His answer, he would not have gone away sad and grieved, but instead would have challenged or contended with the Lord as the Pharisees did.

---

1. We would do well not to limit our application of these verses to a man's struggle with temporal riches. Far more than just silver and gold goes into a man's decision to reject eternal life.

What this young man understood unequivocally was that to take Jesus at His word would mean that he would have to change from his present state. The young man, in that moment, grasped that there must be paired with his affirmative response, a transformation that would redefine him. He must, out of necessity to the invitation, leave the place where he encountered Jesus and move to an altogether different place. Not just different in location or even different in vocation, but an altogether different realm; different in character and makeup; different in design and purpose. (Isaiah 55:9; Luke 18:27; John 8:23; 18:36). The young man contemplated the necessary transformation in form and in substance. It was his appreciation and understanding of this necessity that led him to weigh his world in the balance and choose to decline the Lord's invitation and stay with what he knew. Even Nicodemus, the teacher of Israel, did not reach this level of understanding. (John 3:9-10).

What I know today about this young man is that he sought out the Lord and His opinion on a matter that was very important to him; eternal life. And the response he gave to the Lord was not argumentative, dismissive, or superficial, but it was based upon a deliberate and right understanding of the answer Jesus gave to his question. What the Lord has taught me through this young man's life is the place of *understanding* with regard to the words He speaks.

"*....come, follow Me!*" Regardless of what words may precede them, the Lord invites all men with these words. For some, the invitation may be preceded by the words "*go forth from your country and from your father's house*" or *"you will conceive in your womb and bear a son, and you shall name Him Jesus"* or *"I have put My words in your mouth. You shall speak all these words to them, but they will not listen to you"* (Genesis 12:1; Luke 1:31; Jeremiah 1:9; 7:27). For others, it may be after He comes by and throws His mantle on you or fills your nets to overflowing with fish. (1 Kings 19:19; Mark 1:17). For me, it was *"What you are doing is not of Me. Come, follow Me."* Regardless of how He speaks the invitation, for all of mankind, what He speaks means the same thing; "Come, be transformed!" It is necessary to have understanding of what He speaks.

While the young man from Mark 10 rejected the Lord's invitation, he nevertheless understood it. He knew what it would mean to agree with the Lord on what He said. He understood that to truly follow after the Lord would mean the end of him and the world that he knew. At once, he comprehended that it would be more than simply keeping commandments. It would mean a personal and real transformation. It was something he knowingly was unwilling to do and so he walked away. Although his response to the Lord is not unique, it is nonetheless a response that would be in stark contrast to the multitudes of people who followed after Him without any understanding of the personal cost of doing so or of what was required to enter the kingdom of God.

Filled with Emptiness

The sixth chapter of the Gospel of John records the account of Jesus feeding the multitude. It begins with

Jesus healing the lame man at Bethesda. (John 5:2-9). Because of the signs that Jesus was performing, large crowds followed Him as He traveled from there to the far shore of the Sea of Galilee (John 6:1-2). When Jesus saw the multitudes coming to Him, He asked His disciples where they could buy bread enough to feed the people. His disciples told Him they had not enough money to feed such a large crowd. Then one of His disciples said there was a boy in the crowd with five barley loaves and two fish. Jesus instructed His disciples to have the people sit down. He then gave thanks and distributed from the two fish and five loaves until all that were present were filled. Afterwards, Jesus instructed the disciples to gather up the leftovers. Twelve baskets of barley loaves were collected. *"When the people saw [this] sign which He had performed, they said, "This is truly the Prophet who is to come into the world"* (v. 14).

After the people ate, Jesus withdrew to the mountain alone (v.15). As evening approached, His disciples got into boats and traveled by sea to Capernaum. (v.v. 16-17). The next day when the people saw that neither Jesus nor His disciples were present at the place where they ate the bread, they followed after Him and they too went to Capernaum. When they found Jesus He said to them,

> *"Truly, truly, I say to you, you seek Me, not because you saw signs, but because you ate of the loaves and were filled. Do not work for the food which perishes, but for the food which endures to eternal life, which the Son of Man will give to you, for on Him the Father, God, has set His seal"* (v.v. 26-27).

At this point, the peoples' lack of understanding as to the things Jesus was doing and saying is evident. They observed His works at Jerusalem, at the shore of the Sea of Galilee, and at places prior, yet repeatedly asked Him for a sign so that they may see and believe (John 6:30). By the hand of God they ate and were filled, and yet they were completely empty. They had a carnal understanding, which is no understanding at all. It was founded in the temporal things of the world and not the eternal things of the Spirit. They possessed no appreciation for the meaning of what they heard or saw from Jesus. Yet, that did not prevent them from continuing after Him as He went from place to place.

It was in this environment that we see the Lord very literally bring them to a place of understanding, for He knew that their *following after* Him was not unto eternal life. He began by saying, *"For the bread of God is that which comes down out of heaven, and gives life to the world"* (v. 33). When the people answered by saying, *"Give us this bread"* Jesus said, *"I am the bread....If anyone eats of this bread, he will live forever; and the bread also which I will give for the life of the world is My flesh"* (v.v. 34-35, 51). Jesus then further explained,

> *"Truly, truly, I say to you, unless you eat the flesh of the Son of Man and drink His blood, you have no life in yourselves. He who eats My flesh and drinks My blood has eternal life, and I will raise him up on the last day. For My flesh is true food, and My blood is true drink. He who eats My flesh and drinks My blood abides in Me, and I in him" (v.v. 53-56).*

The Jews who heard Him speak these words began to argue with one another, saying, "*How can this man give us His flesh to eat*" (v. 52)? Even some of His disciples heard these words and said, "*This is a difficult statement; who can listen to it*" (v. 60)?

Finally, the people were at the place of understanding, though not voluntarily. For some time now they had followed after Jesus wherever He went. They watched and observed and heard as He did and said whatever His Father had instructed Him to do or say. Despite seeing and hearing, they lacked understanding. They knew His acts, but they did not know Him. To know Him is to love Him. To love Him is to obey Him. To obey Him you must understand Him. They never understood that in order to truly follow after the Lord, they would have to be transformed from what they were. They were blind to the necessity that their lives would have to come to an end. They lacked an appreciation for what was required to enter the kingdom of God.

As a result of Jesus bringing them to a place of understanding the words He spoke, many of His disciples withdrew and were not walking with Him anymore (v. 66). Just to make sure that He was understood by all, He then turned to the twelve and said, "*You do not want to go away also, do you?*" One of His disciples answered Him, "*Lord, to whom shall we go? You have words of eternal life. We have believed and have come to know that You are the Holy One of God*" (v.v. 67-69).

Enter Through
The Narrow Gate

In the person of the rich young ruler we found a man who understood the words of the Lord and chose to not follow after Him. In the persons of the multitude of John 6 we found a people who followed after the Lord, but had no understanding of His words or His actions. Because they lacked understanding, their following after Him was not unto eternal life. So in that sense they were no better off than the rich young ruler.

There is however a following after that leads to eternal life. It is a following after that is the result of understanding the Lord's words. It is the place where *understanding* and *following after* unite. (See Revelation 14:1-5).

The Scripture records a number of times when this divine union took place. In each instance, the Lord's words were understood, and the hearer <u>affirmatively</u> responded to His invitation fully aware that they must leave their lives behind and proceed with Him wherever He led. (2 Corinthians 5:17). Such an understanding was possessed by Andrew and his brother Simon Peter, and James and his brother John. (John 6:68). Not only did these brothers leave family and vocation (Matthew 4:18-22), but for Andrew and John, they left the company of John the Baptist, for the Messiah had come and the forerunner was finished. (John 1:40). Such was also the understanding of the Roman centurion who beckoned the Jewish rabbi, whom he called *Lord*, to heal his paralyzed servant. (Matthew 8:5-10). And so too for the man with the withered hand, who stood in the synagogue among accusing brethren and obeyed the words, *"Stretch out your hand"* (Luke 6:10)!

Make no mistake, when these and others, like Noah, Moses, Rahab, Elisha, Esther, and Gideon responded affirmatively to the Lord, they did so knowing full well that the person they were at that moment was to be no more. They did not consider that their decision to follow the Lord *might* lead to their death. They understood that their decision to follow the Lord *was* their death, and they followed nonetheless.

The truth of this understanding is demonstrated in none other than Jesus Himself, who,

> *"[A]lthough He existed in the form of God, did not regard equality with God a thing to be grasped, but emptied Himself, taking the form of a bond-servant, and being made in the likeness of men. Being found in appearance as a man, He humbled Himself by becoming obedient to the point of death, even death on a cross"* (Philippians 2:6-8).

Do you really believe that Jesus thought that coming to earth as a man would *lead* to His death? No, He did not think that! Emptying Himself of His equality with God and coming to earth *was* His death, and that death (complete surrender) allowed the Father to live His will in and through His Son. For the Son, that would mean many deaths; daily deaths.

The Apostle Paul expressed his own understanding of this reality to the church in Philippi when he wrote,

"I count all things to be loss in view of the surpassing value of knowing Christ Jesus my Lord, for whom I have suffered the loss of all things, and count them but rubbish so that I may gain Christ" (Philippians 3:8).

And to the churches of Galatia when he said,

"For through the Law I died to the Law, so that I might live to God. I have been crucified with Christ; and it is no longer I who live, but Christ lives in me; and the life which I now live in the flesh I live by faith in the Son of God" (Galatians 2:19-20).

The thing that is shared among all of the people that understand the meaning of the Lord's words and follow after Him nonetheless is that they see life, not in themselves or where they are, but in God and God alone. To follow the Lord as the Lord intends to be followed means a complete and utter transformation of whom and what a man is. There must be an essential change, a conversion, not just in word or thought, but in substance and character, that is manifested in action. (Luke 9:23).

Jesus said, *"Enter through the narrow gate; for the gate is wide and the way is broad that leads to destruction, and there are many who enter through it. For the gate is small and the way is narrow that leads to life, and there are few who find it"* (Matthew 7:13-14).

If entering the kingdom of God is the goal; if obtaining eternal life is the aspiration; then we should do what is necessary to enter in. It is not enough to come near. It is not enough to simply understand, nor is it enough to blindly follow after. We need to understand what the Lord means when He says, "Come, follow Me." Otherwise, our following is in vain and our goal is not reached.

The magnitude of this truth is revealed in Jesus' parable of the wedding feast. There He compared the kingdom of heaven to a wedding feast or a big dinner. The man giving the feast called out to all those who were invited saying *"Come, to the wedding feast"* (Matthew 22:4). But those called began to make excuses, one saying, *"I have bought a piece of land and I need to go out and look at it; please consider me excused."* Another one said, *"I have bought five yoke of oxen, and I am going to try them out; please consider me excused."* Still another said, *"I have married a wife, and for that reason I cannot come"* (Luke 14:18-20). The man then went to the streets and called all, both evil and good, so that the wedding hall was filled with guests. (Matthew 22:9-10). But when the man walked among the guests he noticed a guest who was not properly dressed. He asked the guest, "How did you come in here without wedding clothes?" The guest was unable to respond. The man then ordered the guest to be bound and thrown out, saying, *"For many are called, but few are chosen"* (v.v. 11-14).

In this parable about the kingdom of God, those who were called who gave excuses not to attend are akin to the rich young ruler who knowingly rejected the invitation to come. They understood the invitation, and even knew of the man giving the dinner. Yet, they were unwilling to change their lives around so as to attend his feast. Those good and evil, found in the streets that came when invited are akin to the multitude of John 6. They responded to the invitation and for good reason; it was freely offered and there would be food and drink. However, they came unaware of the requirements to attend. The man without wedding clothes represents the multitude that follows after without understanding. In the end, he is bound and thrown into the darkness. It probably would have been better for him if he, like those who made excuse, never attended the feast.

Today, the Lord says "Come." He invites all men to follow after Him. What will be your response to His calling? Will you reject His invitation? Will you accept it, because He asked? Or will you understand the invitation and do what is required to attend the feast? May your response be the result of understanding and following after Him.

✦

Chapter 16

AT THE END OF DISOBEDIENCE

Scripture Reading:

"If anyone loves Me, he will keep My word; and My Father will love him, and We will come to him and make Our abode with him. He who does not love Me does not keep My words..." (John 14:23-24).

"No one who abides in Him sins; no one who sins has seen Him or knows Him..... No one who is born of God practices sin, because His seed abides in him; and he cannot sin, because he is born of God" (1 John 3:6, 9).

When the Lord instructed me to write this chapter, I was immediately reminded of a counseling session I had a number of years ago. It was with a pastor who wanted to meet with me for prayer. I had been only briefly acquainted with him through our discipleship ministry at the church. I had no idea the reason for his visit before he arrived for our meeting. When he arrived he was visibly nervous and somewhat anxious. Yet he had a sense of expectation. After a short greeting he asked me to pray for him and to intercede for his situation. He informed me that within a matter of days he would lose his house in foreclosure. He told me he was several months behind on his mortgage payments and saw no means or method to get even. He said he was desperate and in need of God's intervention to save his house from being taken away from him.

As he shared his dilemma, the Lord reminded me of a lesson He taught me some years before. The Lord then instructed me to ask the pastor a question; a question, the answer to which the Lord already knew. So I asked, "Did the Lord tell you to buy this house?" As I asked the question, the pastor's body language and facial expression changed. His eyes closed somewhat and he went from standing tall on both feet, to standing slumped on one foot more than the other. I could tell he was both disturbed and disappointed at the question. He delayed in answering, so I asked again, "Did the Lord tell you to buy this house?" He replied, "I did not ask Him about it."

I then said, "So you are here asking me to pray to God to help you save your house when you never sought to know His will concerning the house, nor did He ever instruct you to buy it? I am sorry pastor, I cannot and I will not." I then began to share with him the lesson that the Lord taught me. In short, the lesson was that wherever I find myself and whatever I am doing in that place and at that time, must be as a result of the Lord speaking or directing me. In that way I keep from sin and, regardless of the circumstances, I know that He has led me to that place and that He *is* leading me through it. I shared with the pastor that I strive to find myself only where the Lord leads and nowhere else. I strive to do His will, not my own. If I sin by doing my own will and find myself alone and away from God, I immediately stop and return to Him.

I concluded by telling the pastor again that I could not pray as he requested because it was his will, not God's will for him to have the house. It was God's will however, for him to turn from his sin and turn to God. I encouraged him to stop where he was and stop what he was doing. I admonished him that God is not concerned about his house, but about his heart. This is not what the pastor expected to hear or wanted to hear. We ended our meeting and he went his way.

Over the years I have had many such encounters. In each one of those encounters the Lord has had me ask the same or similar question as the one I posed to the pastor. In nearly every encounter the response was the same; "I have not asked Him" or "He never said anything." One such encounter was a young couple who wanted me to perform their wedding ceremony. They never sought the Lord for His will before deciding to marry. I did not do the wedding. (Matthew 19:6).

In another encounter, a couple sought to save their struggling marriage through counseling. During our session together I learned that the Lord specifically told each of them not to marry the other. Yet, they each disregarded what the Lord spoke and proceeded to marry. Now after several years they were struggling to keep it together. I told them to repent and ask the Lord what He wanted them to do going forward because where they were at that moment was in complete disobedience. Apart from that, I would do no more counseling for them. (Psalm 127:1).

In addition, a number of people have asked that I pray for God's blessing and favor over a new business venture, an upcoming ministry endeavor, a career path change, or an impending medical procedure. In each instance I learned that God was not asked, nor did He speak on the matter before a decision was made or an action was taken. (James 4:13-17). In each of these instances I did not pray as I was requested to pray. Instead, I warned each person of their sin and encouraged them to stop and turn to God.

The Gospel of Luke chapter 15 records a story that Jesus shared while in the presence of tax collectors, Pharisees, scribes, and irreligious Jews. Unfortunately, this story has been traditionally titled *"The Prodigal Son."* It is unfortunate because this titling, like much of the subtitling found in the Bible is erroneous and very misleading.   I point out that the words of Jesus as recorded in this Gospel account do not include the use of the word *prodigal*. In fact, the story itself was not told so as to illustrate reckless or wasteful spending behavior by a son, but to reveal a much greater truth that I will share shortly.

Just for the record, when God spoke to the prophets and apostles and those prophets and apostles recorded what He said, He did not give them subtitles to include in their written account. All of the subtitles found in the Bible were added by man, mostly during the Middle Ages when the original writings of the prophets and apostles were being translated into different languages and being printed for mass production, as the Bible. The titling of the Prodigal Son story is just one of these subtitling occurrences.

So, Jesus tells those gathered around him of a man who had two sons, the younger of which demanded from him the part of his wealth that was to be that son's inheritance. Consequently, the father divided his wealth and gave his son his part and the son then left for a distant place and spent the wealth on his every desire. When his money had come to an end the young man was forced to work in the fields and eat with the animals just to survive. Eventually, the young man realized that in his father's house, even his father's workers had better conditions than those in which he found himself.

Therefore, he purposed to return to his father's house and repent of his sin and ask his father if he could simply work for him as a hired man. He started for his father's house. As the young man approached the house, yet even still far off, the father saw him and ran to the young man and embraced him. The son then said to his father, *"Father, I have sinned against heaven and in your sight; I am no longer worthy to be called your son"* (vv. 18-19). The father responded by instructing his slaves to place upon his son the best robe, a ring and sandals; and then to kill the fattened calf and prepare for a celebration, saying, *"for this son of mine was dead and has begun to live, and was lost and has been found"* (vv. 24, 32).

Again, most likely influenced by the use of subtitles and additionally by a continuing reliance upon the teachings and traditions of man, the conventional Christian reading or studying of this story tends to focus on the foolish spending behavior of the younger son and the outcome, particularly the father's longing for and love for the son, and how the son was welcomed back into the father's house with lovingkindness. It is read in much the same way that the Book of Job is read. In Job's case, everyone recalls Job's plight at the hands of Satan, the onerous advice given Job by his friends, and that in the end God restored Job's fortune twofold. (Job 42:10). But this conventional reading of these stories neglects their intended and principal purpose, that is, to illustrate to mankind that relationship with God begins with repentance from sin, with an ending of disobedience. If in reading the story of the father and his sons, you focus on the reckless spending actions of the son; or, if you focus simply on what God did at the end of either story, [in the story of the prodigal, the father is representative of God] then you miss that what He did with the man He did because something on man's part preceded God's response. In the account of Job and in the account of the younger son, a man repented of his sin and turned to God. It was then that God restored the fortune or welcomed the son home.

Ninety-nine out of one hundred Christians would tell you that Job was in right-standing with God before Satan came a calling. That is a misguided understanding of the account. A proper understanding of the book reveals that Job was filled with self-righteousness and was actually not in proper relationship with God despite all of his religiosity. God knew this from the outset and in His mercy put in motion events that would bring Job to see for himself the deception in which he lived. With God's mercy, Job finally saw what God already knew. Job repented and for the first time in his life, he knew God rightly. (Job 42:1-6). For a more in depth look into the life of Job see *The War of the Lord.*

Now, those same ninety-nine would also contend that the "prodigal son" was in proper relationship with his father before he left on his journey and that he simply had his relationship restored upon his return from temporary debauchery. This too is a misguided understanding of this account. In reality, the son had no relationship with the father prior to his return. He had at most a relationship with the *things* of the father that he considered to be his own. The son demonstrated no regard, nor respect, nor love for the father. We begin to get a glimpse into the son's true condition when the son returns home and the father says, *"This son of mine was dead and has begun to live"* (Luke 15:32).

Again, a conventional (carnal) reading of this account would characterize the son's life prior to his departure as *living*. Yet, the father describes that time period as his son being *dead*. Most believe that the young man was alive and died and then was made alive again. That is not correct. The young man was dead, and after he repented of his sin and returned, he *began to live*. His existence prior to his repentance was equated to death. (Matthew 8:22). Like every man, he was born into death. (Ephesians 4:17-24; 5:6-9).

Now, when the young man finally came to his senses, he expressed a longing to simply be with his father, even if it was as a worker and not a son. When he returned to his father's house, he finds joy in his father and not the things of his father. Upon his return, he possessed a joy he never even knew existed prior to his repentance. Like Job, what the younger son came to understand was that the relationship that he thought he had with the father/God, in fact did not exist. (Job 42:1-6).

As the Scripture verses at the top of our reading establish, a relationship with God *begins* at the end of disobedience. In other words, unless a man lives before God without sin he can have no relationship with God. (1 John 3:6, 9). That is not to say that he cannot have a relationship with Jesus. The man can have a relationship with the Messiah and Savior. He just cannot have a relationship with God the Father. Jesus can and will embrace the sinner. He can and has taken the sin of man upon Himself. There is no sinner who comes to the Lord who will be turned away. (Luke 5:32). But the same is not true of God the Father. No sin can come before the Almighty, even if that sin is carried by His Son. (Psalm 15; Ezekiel 28:14-16). Remember, when Jesus bore the sin of mankind upon Himself, the Father turned His gaze from the Son. Jesus, aware of this, cried out, "*My God, My God, why have You forsaken Me*" (Matthew 27:46). Jesus came to earth to give man the way to have relationship with His God (John 14:6); the forgiveness of sin and the call to stop sinning. Do not underestimate the importance of the words He spoke at the first:

"*The kingdom of God is at hand; repent*"
(Mark 1:15).

From man's infancy, obedience to God has been *the* condition for a relationship with Him. (Genesis 2:16; 3:17; Ezekiel 28:15-16). If man hears and follows the voice of God he has life; otherwise he has death. (1 Kings 9:4-7; Revelation 2:4-5; 3:2-3, 5, 14-22). Life is simply to know God and Jesus Christ, His Son. (John 17:3). To know Him is to love Him. To love Him is to obey Him. To obey Him is to abide in Him and Him in you.

Death is separation from Life (Romans 6:23) and is the fruit of disobedience. (Matthew 25:41-46; Hebrews 3:16-1). Disobedience is *not* doing what God commands. Disobedience is also *doing* what God has not commanded. God is always calling man to depart from the way of death. (Matthew 4:17; John 8:11). When man lives his life by what God speaks, God Himself lives in him, he is in relationship with God, and he has Life. (John 14:23). When man lives his life independent of God's government, directly or indirectly, he is in sin and therefore not in relationship with God (John 14:24a).

This reality presents a dilemma for almost all Christians because they believe that a relationship with God is established through association or a decision of allegiance that is believed to coincide with a religious act like water baptism, a profession of faith, a prayer of salvation, the baptism of the Holy Spirit, or whatever else may be out there that religion declares qualifies you to assert a relationship to God. This is further confused by the belief that nothing can interfere with such a relationship once it is formed. Coupled with these lies is the belief that all sin, past, present, and future is washed away for the one who has made *that* decision. Working together, these religious beliefs lead a person to mistakenly rest in a relationship that does not exist. (Jeremiah 7:1-11; 1 Corinthians 7:19; Romans 2:28-29).

The eternal consequences of such a belief structure are quite shocking to say the least. The children of Israel, specifically during the times of the exodus, the judges and the kings, experienced the results of association or allegiance to God without a corresponding obedience. To see the full effect of their experience, see *The Divine Intention – a Journey to ... Salvation.*

And so, a relationship with God is established through obedience, not through any religious action, association, or declaration, even if that action, association, or declaration includes Jesus or His name. Jesus taught as much during His discourse as recorded in chapters five through seven of the Gospel of Matthew. There He stated that only those who do the will of the Father will enter heaven. During His discourse He spoke of those who professed an association or declared an allegiance to Him by calling Him "Lord" and proclaiming their works done in His name. To those, Jesus responded by saying, *"Depart from Me, for I never knew you"* (Matthew 7:21).

By His own life Jesus demonstrated that relationship with God is established through obedience, not association. The life He lived was not lived by inherent divine attributes (Philippians 2:6-7), but lived by imparted divine attributes. (Luke 4:18-19). Moreover, Jesus' exaltation by the Father was not because He existed with the Father before coming to earth. His exaltation by the Father was due to His absolute obedience to the Father while on the earth. (Philippians 2:8-9). Jesus confirmed the character of His relationship with the Father when He said,

> *"For I did not speak on My own initiative, but the Father Himself who sent Me has given Me a commandment as to what to say and what to speak. I know that His commandment is eternal life; therefore the things I speak, I speak just as the Father has told Me"* (John 12:49-50).

Jesus' relationship with His Father, a relationship founded upon obedience, is further illustrated in the account of His temptation. Three times Satan challenges Jesus' relationship with God by tempting Him to disobey and three times Jesus proves His relationship to the Father, as Son, through His obedience to the Father. (Luke 4:3-12; 1 John 3:6, 9). This is in stark contrast to the ending of the relationship that Adam had with God.

Genesis 3 records how Satan tempted Adam and Eve to disobey what the Lord had spoken. The result of the temptation is well known; the consequences not so much. Because Adam failed to obey the words of God, he lost his relationship with God. Consequently, man lost his relationship to God and that relationship could only be restored through the obedience of Another. (Romans 5:12, 19).

God desires a relationship with all men. He wants that none should perish, but that all would trust in Him and Him alone. He gave Himself to man to arrive at that end. Yet, it is only the man who obeys the voice of the Lord that enters into that relationship. Once again we can look to the sons of Israel to see how this truth played out in their time and how it may guide us in ours.

As recorded in the Book of Judges, the sons of Israel moved in and out of cycles of obeying and disobeying the voice of the Lord. When they disregarded His voice He sent them into oppression and servitude. This happened as the sons of Israel continually longed for the things of the world and desired to be like the peoples around them instead of longing after their God and being the people He had called them to be. (Judges 3:1-8; 4:1-3; 6:1-6).

While in these times of oppression Israel suffered greatly and in some instances those individuals who disregarded the counsel of the Lord perished and a new generation arose who would listen to and follow the Lord.

(Psalm 107:10-12). The sons of Israel then returned to their God and were freed from their oppressors. This cycle of rebellion continued for generations, even unto the days of Jeremiah, before the Babylonian captivity, when the sons of Israel spurned the Lord yet again and instead desired to turn to Egypt for safety from the Babylonians. The prophet rebuked Israel saying,

"So I have told you today, but you have not obeyed the Lord your God, even in whatever He has sent me to tell you. Therefore you should now clearly understand that you will die by the sword, by famine and by pestilence, in the place where you wish to go to reside" (Jeremiah 42:21-22).

Obedience, not professions; substance, not form is required to know and be known by God. If you read Paul's individual letters in their entirety instead of simply reading fragments of the letters, you see clearly that the closing emphasis of the letters is the Apostle admonishing and encouraging the saints to cease from sin. In his letter to the Galatians, after challenging their inclination to return to the Law after experiencing grace through Christ (Galatians 1:6-7; 3:1-5; 4:21; 5:1), Paul warned the saints about the perils of *continuing* in the ways of the flesh (5:13, 16-21, 24-26; 6:8-9).

To the church in Ephesus Paul began by sharing with them the mystery of Christ which had been hidden in God throughout the ages, but that in God's time was made known to him by revelation from the Father. (Ephesians 1:9, 3:3-9). He encouraged them in the grace by which they have been saved, through their faith in Christ. (1:4-5, 7-8; 2:5, 8). Then he closed his letter to the church by reproving the saints against *continuing* to walk *"as the Gentiles also walk, in the futility of their mind, being darkened in their understanding"* (4:17-18). He instructs the church to *"lay aside the old self...and put on the new self, which in the likeness of God has been created in righteousness and holiness of the truth"* (4:22-32; 5:3-29; 6:1-9).

To the Philippians Paul expressed his confidence in God, that the work which the Lord began in the church He would perfect. (Philippians 1:6; 2:13). In that regard, the Apostle instructed the church to *"conduct itself in a manner worthy of the gospel of Christ"* and do nothing from selfish ambition or personal interest, *"but with humility of mind"* and a surrendered heart to God, regard another as more important than oneself. (2:3-4).

Paul charged the church at Colossae to *"set [their] mind on the things above, not on the things that are on earth* [and] *to consider the members of [their] earthly body as dead to immorality, impurity, passion, evil desire, and greed"* (Colossians 3:2, 5). He instructed them to set *"aside anger, wrath, malice, slander, and abusive speech from [their] mouth, and ... to put on a heart of compassion, kindness, humility, gentleness and patience"* (vv. 8, 12). These same admonitions were given to the saints in Corinth (who were not walking in truth) and Thessalonica (who were actually walking in truth), for their correction and encouragement, and to Titus for his use in instructing the different churches that he visited.

(1 Corinthians 1:11; 3:3; 5:1-3; 6:9-10, 18; 10:14; 1 Thessalonians 4:1-8; Titus 1:5, 13).

⸺ ⟡ ⸺

As controversial as this all may sound, the most troubling aspect is not that relationship with God begins when disobedience ends; that is simply the truth. No, the most troubling aspect is that because of a deceived heart man can live his whole life in sin and therefore out of relationship with God, and the whole time be unaware of his sinfulness and his separation from God.

Shortly after I started to write this chapter, one of my spiritual sisters received a dream from the Lord. It is with her consent that I share this dream. I include it here because of its relevance to what the Lord is saying.

Her dream began with a bright sunny day and her standing in front of a beautiful Victorian-style house. There was an "Open House" in progress and so she entered, keenly aware that she was being accompanied by the Lord. Once inside she observed that there were rooms filled with wonderful things, and not just filled, but overly filled. For example, the first room she entered was like a parlor. It had not one, but three pianos. While in the parlor, she noticed a lady standing next to one of the pianos. She saw the lady take a sheet of music from atop the piano. My sister took note and moved to the next room. The second room was filled with fine Victorian china. In the room there were several ladies sitting at a table, using some of the china to have tea and cookies.

They were not simply using it. It was as though they were awestruck as they used the china.

As my sister continued walking throughout the house she returned to the parlor where she was about to sit down and play one of the pianos. It is then that the Lord said to her, "*No [my child], let's move on.*" She, without hesitation followed the Lord's instruction which led her down a hallway toward the front door. In the hallway was a man looking at a cabinet filled with Victorian-style jewelry. The man seemed to be mesmerized by the jewelry and had taken some of it into his hand as she approached. She warned the man against doing so, but he paid no attention to her words. She then exited the house. The first thing she noticed upon exiting the house was that it was no longer sunny. In fact it was dark and gloomy. After walking away from the house a short distance she turned back to the house. Instead of a beautiful Victorian-style house she saw an old, broken-down, haunted-type of a house. The dream ended.

The Lord revealed the following as it concerns the dream:

The Victorian house is this present age; the world in which we live, the world into which we are born. The rooms of the house and all that they contain are all that this world contains; tangible and intangible. All are invited into the house however, what you do once inside reveals your relationship to the house and its contents. Those that take hold of it, physically or emotionally, become ensnared by it, completely unaware of their captivity. Such was the case with the woman who took the sheet music. At some point she entered the house and at some point thereafter she took hold of the sheet music as she walked through the parlor. What she remained unaware of was that she could not leave the room. The same was true for the women having tea as well as the man holding the jewelry. Because they had taken hold of the contents of the house or stopped to use its contents, they were trapped, but their desire and fascination with the things in the house prevented them from seeing the ruse.

It is important to note that each room contained something that was desirable to my sister. The music, the china and the jewelry were all high on her list of desirable things. However, those desires remained always submitted to the Lord. Even when she saw what was desirable to her, she never allowed those desires to distract her away from the Lord's voice.

Through the dream the Lord is communicating to us that man lives entangled in sin unaware. Though man is placed in this world at birth, man is not to be a part of this world; he is called away by God to the place where he belongs; in the Lord. However, man is captivated and ensnared by this present world and completely oblivious to his condition. Worse still, because of the darkness that *is* religion, man is taught by evil men, who proclaim to know God, that the house and its contents are God's gift to man; the answer to a prayer and the desires of a heart. In that way religion; Christianity in particular, insures that man will be taken captive by the things of the world. It does this by deceptively labeling that which is forbidden by God, as being that which is freely given and readily available to you from God. Sounds very similar to the struggle Adam and Eve faced in the Garden. This is all the result of a heart that is hardened to sin. It is the deceitfulness of the heart of man that allows him to live in sin unaware and because of religion, allow him to live in sin while believing he is holy.

The heart of man is a paradox. There is nothing like it. For with it man can either draw near to God or run from Him. (Luke 10:27; Matthew 15:8). The heart of man is both the soil in which the Lord plants His word (Jeremiah 31:33; Matthew 13:19) and the place from which all sorts of evil comes forth. (Matthew 15:18-19). It can treasure the things of earth or the things of heaven (Matthew 6:19-21). It can be tender and trusting of the Lord (Proverbs 3:5, Ephesian 4:32) or it can be hard and hate Him (2 Chronicles 36:11-13, Luke 16:13). Despite all of the contradictions of the heart, two things are certain: *"a good tree cannot produce bad fruit, nor can a bad tree produce good fruit;"* and only God can understand it and only He can weigh it. (Matthew 7:18; 12:33-37; Psalm 33:15; Proverbs 21:2). Man is no match for it because with all of its craftiness, the heart of man can mislead even itself. (Proverbs 16:1-2). It is the hardened heart that runs to evil and it is the hardened heart that does not see it.

It was undoubtedly an unbelieving heart in the sons of Israel that brought upon them the wrath of God. (Hebrews 3:12-19). Yet, it was their deceived hearts that enabled them to declare their holiness before Him. (Number 16:1-3). It was a rebellious and insubordinate heart that caused King Saul to directly disobey the commandment of the Lord. Yet, it was his deluded heart that led him to plead his innocence before the Judge. (1 Samuel 15:10-28). It was a heart of lawlessness that brought a people to speak and act in the name of the Lord (Matthew 7:20-22). Yet, it was a misled heart that justified itself before God.

In the case of the visiting pastor, he believed he was living holy and thereby in relationship to God by praying or asking for prayer concerning his predicament. Yet, his predicament was in the first place the result of his sin (his disobedience). The same was true of the "Christian" couple who came in for "Christian" marriage counseling. They believed themselves to be in right-standing with the Lord [because prior professions and declarations], and they sought His touch in their lives. Yet, it was the hardness of a deceived heart that pressed forward in disobedience in the face of the Lord's command.

The same is true for all of those who live their life without regard for the Lord or His word. Their faith is based upon a belief that they are in relationship with the Lord, yet their never-ending disobedience is the evidence that they do not even know Him. They trust in what they have declared, unaware that what they have declared is not true in them. The deceived heart is always in disobedience and therefore in sin, and the sinful heart is always separated from God. Again, what is true is that relationship with the Father is found only at the end of man's disobedience.

I want to conclude with this; that forgiveness of sin is available to all men. (Luke 24:47; Acts 10:43; Colossians 1:14). This forgiveness of sin is through Jesus Christ alone, who was given freely by God the Father. (John 3:16). Whether or not you are religious, spiritual, non-religious, or even call yourself Christian, if you are living in sin, the solution is simple; repent; stop where you are and stop what you are doing and turn to God. He will receive you unconditionally and without regard to your transgression because of the shed blood of His Son. But you must turn, you must repent; and you must put an end to disobedience. This is the message of the kingdom.

Finally, it may be helpful to know that there is a feeling of hopelessness that accompanies the time leading up to true repentance. (Isaiah 6:4-5; Jonah 3; Luke 5:1-11). It is the hopelessness that is characteristic of sin and death. It is the hopelessness that is brought to you by God Himself. (Judges 2:14; John 3:9; 6:60-69). The hopelessness increases as repentance draws near. You become more aware of this hopelessness as you become more aware of your sinfulness.

It is in this environment of hopelessness that a man has opportunity to choose Life. (Genesis 4:6-8). This choice is simply the freewill choice to trust the Lord in all things and at all times and not trust yourself or anything else or anyone else. Once you chose Life, the hopelessness is extinguished and completely replaced with the joy of knowing Him who called you from the beginning.

But, this same hopelessness also has the power to prevent you from repenting by causing you to either disregard your sin as not being sin, thereby quieting the hopelessness and providing a false sense of peace, or by leading you to a place of sadness and aimlessness, and at times even remorse, but a place that is short of true repentance. (1 Corinthians 5; Mark 10:17-22). A hardened heart feels no hopelessness as a result of its sin and a saddened but non-repentant heart focuses on oneself and not God. However, do not be deceived,

> *"God is not mocked [He will not allow Himself to be ridiculed, nor treated with contempt nor allow His precepts to be scornfully set aside]; for whatever a man sows, this and this only is what he will reap"* (Galatians 6:7). Amplified Bible.

If man choses to not repent he will pay the wages of sin. (Romans 6:23).

✦

Chapter 17

*T*he *C*ulmination

Scripture Reading:

"Jesus said to them, "My food is to do the will of Him who sent Me and to accomplish His work" (John 4:34).

"For judgment I came into this world, so that those who do not see may see, and that those who see may become blind" (John 9:39).

At all times they are giving Glory to God

Within a matter of days after leading the sons of Israel out from under the oppressive hand of Pharaoh, Moses arrived with the people in the wilderness of Shur. There they found no water. Then they came to the bitter waters of Marah and the congregation of Israel began to grumble against Moses. So Moses cried out to the Lord and the Lord responded, and *"showed him a tree"* and instructed him to throw it into the waters. Moses obeyed the Lord's command and God was pleased; *"the waters became sweet"* and the people drank (Exodus 15:25).

A short time later, when Moses and the congregation of Israel arrived at Rephidim after journeying from the wilderness of Sin, the people again had no water to drink. Again they grumbled against Moses. So Moses asked the Lord what he should do. The Lord then commanded Moses to take the staff with which he struck the Nile and *"go and strike the rock, and water will come out of it, that the people may drink"* (Exodus 17:4-6). Moses did so. God was pleased and the people drank.

Thereafter, the sons of Israel came to the wilderness of Zin, at Kadesh. They again found no water. The Lord then commanded Moses to *"take the rod... and assemble the congregation and speak to the rock before their eyes, that it may yield its water"* (Numbers 20:8). So Moses took the rod as the Lord had commanded him and assembled the people before the rock. He then lifted up his hand and struck the rock twice with his rod. Water came forth abundantly and the people drank. However, the Lord was not pleased for He said to Moses and Aaron, *"Because you have not believed Me, to treat Me as holy in the sight of the sons of Israel, therefore you shall not bring this assembly into the land which I have given them"* (20:12).

Several months ago one of my brothers in the church asked me, "What then follows grace?" His question was referring to the revelation we received a couple of years prior concerning the purpose and meaning of faith. In short, the revelation we received was that mercy is given by God to all men. This mercy is offered to man in the form of invitations in the ordinary course of life. These invitations are opportunities to believe and trust [have faith in] God. Sadly, it is most probable that these opportunities result in unbelief and therefore sin. (Matthew 7:14).

However, if in any particular opportunity man chooses to believe God, then that belief or faith should result in obedience [the purpose and meaning of faith]. If, in belief and trust, the man obeys, then *grace* [God's power] is supplied by God to accomplish His will in that life. This is not meant to imply that when grace is given that a desired or favorable material change in circumstances will occur. It may, but the primary aim of grace is to bring one into an intimate relationship with God, and that intimacy is intended by God to increase over time with continued obedience.

If, on the other hand, a man's belief or faith does not result in obedience then the purpose of faith is not realized, no grace is supplied, and God's will is not accomplished in that life. This is not meant to imply that a desired or favorable material change in circumstances will *not* occur in a life when a man does not respond to God in obedience. When disobedience occurs, something desired by man very well may come to pass; it is just that it is not God's will (increased intimacy) that is accomplished in such a man. Since, in that instance, there was not obedience born out of faith, it would be as though the man did not believe, and unbelief is sin, and sin separates man from God. (Hebrews 3:18-19).

To fully appreciate and apprehend this revelation it must be understood first that only mercy is given freely to all men. It is given by God out of His abundant love for man. This mercy is manifested by way of the circumstances and situations of everyday life. Some are extraordinary, some are tragic, but most are mundane. Whether extraordinary, tragic, or mundane, it is rare that man recognizes these events as God's mercy being extended. Nevertheless, they are each an invitation to hear and follow Him and His will and not be persuaded or led by the circumstances and situations of the human existence.

Second, faith is not an end in itself. Faith must produce obedience in the one who possesses it. If faith does not result in obedience, that faith amounts to little more than hope and counts for nothing.

Finally, grace is not divine favor or God's lovingkindness. Grace is power; God's power to revive and restore a dead relationship and it is neither free nor unmerited. (Romans 5:12). It is the result of obedience, and to possess it one must pay for it by surrendering all to God and trusting Him to accomplish His will. If, in doing so, He chooses to extend to the obedient one His favor or lovingkindness, then that one is blessed all the more. More information on this subject is available in the chapters entitled, *Faith Perfected* and *What God Thinks*.

So, the question my brother presented was, if in our daily lives there is mercy followed by belief, and that belief produces obedience and that obedience opens the door to grace, "what then follows grace?" My answer was, "Glory follows grace." I did admit to him that although God shared with me the answer, I did not yet understand what that answer meant. I knew however that in His time the Lord would give understanding. Today, I have that understanding.

At all times *"The heavens are telling of the glory of God"* and "[the elements] *are fulfilling His word"* (Psalm 19:1; 148:7-8). At every sunrise and in every whirlwind, the Lord God is given glory. When the stars of the night sky glisten and when the eagle sores in the heavens, the Lord God is given glory. When a leaf falls from the tallest tree of the forest and when a hurricane forms in the seas, the Lord God is given glory. On the other hand, when the Lord God commands the man, saying, *"From any tree of the garden you may eat freely; but from the tree of the knowledge of good and evil you shall not eat"* and the man eats from the tree of the knowledge of good and evil, the Lord is not given glory. (Genesis 2:16-17). Neither is the Lord given glory when the Lord says to the man, *"Speak to the rock"* and the man strikes the rock. Simply put, God receives glory when His word is fulfilled; when His commandment is obeyed; when He is pleased.

With the exception of man, God is glorified by all of creation all of the time. Why? He is glorified because His word is performed without alteration, without fail, and without hesitation. With light and darkness; with wind and rain; with the mountains and the valleys, obedience instead of rebellion is the first and only response to His word and that obedience brings glory to God because His will is accomplished. To illustrate, consider some of the text of Psalm 104,

> [3] *He lays the beams of His upper chambers in the waters; He makes the clouds His chariot; He walks upon the wings of the wind;* [4] *He makes the winds His messengers, flaming fire His ministers.* [5] *He established the earth upon its foundations....*
>
> [6] *The waters were standing above the mountains.* [7] *At [His] rebuke they fled, at the sound of [His] thunder they hurried away.* [8] *The mountains rose; the valleys sank down to the place which [He] established for them.* [9] *[He] set a boundary that they may not pass over, so that they will not return to cover the earth.* [10] *He sends forth springs in the valleys; they flow between the mountains;* [11] *they give drink to every beast of the field; the wild donkeys quench their thirst.* [12] *Beside them the birds of the heavens dwell; they lift up their voices among the branches.* [13] *He waters the mountains from His upper chambers; The earth is satisfied with the fruit of His works.* [14] *He causes the grass to grow for the*

cattle, and vegetation for the labor of man, so that he may bring forth food from the earth....

[19] He made the moon for the seasons; The sun knows the place of its setting. [20] [He] appoints darkness and it becomes night....

[27] ....[All] the beasts of the forest wait for [Him] to give them their food in due season. [28] [He] gives to them, they gather it up; [He] opens [His] hand, they are satisfied with good. [29] [He] hides [His] face, they are dismayed;
[He] takes away their spirit, they expire and return to their dust....

[31] Let the glory of the Lord endure forever; Let the Lord be glad in His works; [32] He looks at the earth, and it trembles; He touches the mountains, and they smoke.

Oh, that this would be the description of man's response to God's will. But sorrowfully it is not.

Given or Retained –
It's Your Choice

With God, glory, His glory, is the supreme issue. (John 12:28). It is the end of His purpose. (1 Peter 4:11). It is the completion of His work. (Isaiah 60:21). It was the purpose of His Son's coming and it is the objective of His return. (John 13:31; 17:1-5). It is what the four living creatures and the twenty-four elders do continuously

(Revelation 4:8-11) and it is what will illuminate the Eternal Dwelling. (Revelation 21:23).

Since glory holds *the* preeminent place in God's universe, it would be to our advantage to seek to grasp its meaning and accomplish its purpose. To that end, we will concentrate on four characteristics of the glory given God by man. In each, I pray we will gain understanding and set ourselves on the path to pleasing the Father. The characteristics are: choice; attribution; origination; and strength.

———————

The Lord God made clear His command to the king regarding the destruction of Amalek when He said,

"Now go and strike Amalek and utterly destroy all that he has, and do not spare him; but put to death both man and woman, child and infant, ox and sheep, camel and donkey" (1 Samuel 15:3).

Following the battle, the prophet came to the king and inquired as to the reason why the Amalekite king was still alive and why Israel was in possession of the spoils of battle. The king, after declaring to the prophet that he had obeyed the command of the Lord, told the man of God that he spared the best of that which was set for destruction so that the people could make a sacrifice to the Lord. (vv. 13-15). The prophet then spoke the disgust and displeasure of the Lord, saying,

Has the Lord as much delight in burnt offerings and sacrifices as in obeying the voice of the Lord? Behold, to

obey is better than sacrifice, and to heed than the fat of rams. For rebellion is as the sin of divination, and insubordination is as iniquity and idolatry. Because you have rejected the word of the Lord, He has also rejected you from being king" (vv. 22-23).

Through the prophet, the Lord then tore the kingdom of Israel from the king and gave it to another. He then destroyed Agag, king of the Amalekites, as He first intended. (Exodus 17:8-16; 1 Samuel 15:28, 33).

In the days of Herod, king of Judea the angel Gabriel came to Nazareth in Galilee and appeared to a young virgin named Mary. She was engaged to marry Joseph of Bethlehem. (Luke 2:4). Gabriel told Mary that the power of God would overshadow her and that she would bear a son whose name would be Jesus. The angel also said that the child would be called the Son of God and that *"His kingdom would have no end"* (Luke 1:26, 27, 31, 35). As astonishing as these words must have sounded to Mary and pondering the consequences they would have upon her life, she answered Gabriel saying, *"[M]ay it be done to me according to your word"* (Luke 1:38). In the appointed time, the Child was born. (Luke 2:6-7). Some thirty-three years later, as they nailed this Child to a cross, a Roman centurion who witnessed Jesus yield up His spirit said, *"Truly this was the Son of God"* (Matthew 27:50, 54).

In the lives of King Saul and the Virgin, we find our first characteristic of the glory that is given to God by man: first and foremost, man must *choose* to give glory to God. Unlike the rest of creation, because God created man with a free will, it requires an intentional act of man to follow after or to turn away from the will of God. To follow after His will is a consequence of man wholly trusting in and believing God. To turn away from His will is a consequence of man trusting in and believing himself. Divine glory emanates only from the former. Saul chose the latter. The Virgin chose better.

In His mercy, the Lord God hid the water from the sons of Israel. He did so, not to harm them, but to bless them; not to make them suffer, but to lead them to the Fountain of Living Water. This was and is the Divine Intention.

In the wilderness of Shur and at Rephidim, the sons of Israel chose to respond to the Lord's invitation with unbelief and complaining, despite having just witnessed the hand of the Lord move mightily against Pharaoh. In their unbelief, Israel rejected God's mercy, sinned against the Lord and had, on that occasion, no avenue to arrive at obedience or to glorify the Lord.

On the other hand, what Moses did in these two instances was choose to glorify the Lord, despite the rebellion of the sons of Israel. He believed and trusted the Lord in these opportunities and his faith resulted in his obedience. In so doing, Moses pleased the Lord in the presence of the congregation. That obedience opened the door to God's grace being supplied and doing what God intended at the first. (*See* Exodus 6:6-8; Deuteronomy 7:6).

Regrettably however, on the occasion that the sons of Israel arrived at Kadesh, Moses joined in the congregation's unbelief. At Kadesh, Moses chose his way. He failed to glorify the Lord. The Lord commanded one thing and Moses did another. The Lord's commandment was not obeyed and therefore, He was not pleased. It is at this point where the truth about grace can be seen. Grace is not the power to produce the miraculous. It is the power to draw closer to a Holy God. Since God hid the water in the first place, He did not need to exercise some divine power to bring it forth. He simply needed to reveal it at His choosing. Moses' obedience or disobedience had less to do with producing the water and more to do with pleasing or displeasing God. Therefore, at Kadesh the people drank, but Moses lost an opportunity to draw closer.

The second characteristic of the glory that is given to God is that such glory given is not attributable to any person other than the one who obeyed. In the case of Moses in the wilderness of Shur and at Rephidim, glory was given by Moses to God by way of his obedience to God's word. God's word was fulfilled and He was pleased. As a by-product, the people received from the hand of God. But the glory that God received was attributed only to Moses and it was only he who grew in intimacy with the Lord. Nothing that the sons of Israel did in those days was born out of faith or resembled obedience to God and it is clear God found no pleasure in them. (*See* Exodus 32:7-10; Hebrews 3:16-19).

We see this same characteristic of glory again in the occasion of Lazarus' resurrection. There, as in all things, Jesus obeyed the Father's word, not being moved by the pressures bearing down upon Him. To the contrary, "*He emptied Himself, taking the form of a bond-servant"* and drew closer to the Father. (Philippians 2:7, 9). In that obedient surrender Jesus glorified His Father. (*See* Matthew 12:18; Mark 1:11; John 17:4). As a by-product of this glory received, God supplied the grace that raised Lazarus from the grave. The people were amazed and [verbally] gave glory to God, but the glory that God received that day was attributed only to Jesus. It was not attributed to Mary (John 11:32), Martha (John 11:39-40), or the Disciples (John 11:16), as they demonstrated only fear, doubt, and unbelief when offered the opportunity to draw closer. Glory given is not a matter of words spoken but of words obeyed.

Our third characteristic is found when we look to the life of the prophet Jeremiah. In his life, we see not only the characteristics of choice and attribution, but of origination as well. Even before the boy left his mother's womb God spoke to him saying,

> *"I have appointed you a prophet to the nations... everywhere I send you, you shall go, and all that I command you, you shall speak"* (Jeremiah 1:5, 7).

When the boy became a young man the Lord came to him saying,

> *"What do you see, Jeremiah?"* And he responded saying, *"I see a rod of an almond tree."* Then the LORD said to him, *"You have seen well, for I am watching over My word to perform it"* (Jeremiah 1:11-12).

That man became the appointed prophet, as he then spoke the words of the Lord to Judah before it was besieged by Babylonian forces and led into captivity. (Jeremiah 2-7).

As the verses above evidence, the purpose of and plan for Jeremiah's life began with God speaking. The prophetic words he spoke to Judah originated from the mouth of God. (John 12:49). This is actually true of all men who glorify the Father, as the glory they give to Him is the result of their obedience to something He did or spoke at the first. (John 5:19). That obedience may be accomplished by speaking, or remaining silent. (Matthew 27:14; Luke 4:21). It may be accomplished by going or staying. (Luke 2:42-43; 8:22). It may be accomplished by blessing or cursing. (Mark 10:13-16; 11:13-14, 21). Regardless of how the obedient action manifests, the obedient action originated with God's command. We have seen this to be true with Jesus, Moses, Jeremiah, Mary, and all who glorify the Father.

Many, even still today, unaware of the requirement of origination, offer strange fire to God believing they are giving Him glory. The glory given to God can <u>never</u> arise from within the man; he cannot desire nor will it; it must flow through him. (*See* Leviticus 10:1-3; 2 Samuel 6:1-7). Therefore, without a command first emanating from God, no obedience can be accomplished and if no obedience, then no glory. The only glory that can be given to God is the glory He Himself initiates.

———————————

I stated previously that the primary aim of grace is to bring one into an intimate relationship with God and that intimacy is intended by God to increase over time with continued obedience. Our fourth characteristic of the glory that is given to God is the characteristic which makes possible that continued obedience.

We have seen that when the Lord God is obeyed, He is pleased. And when He is pleased, He supplies the grace that draws man to Himself, apart from which, no man can draw near. (Jeremiah 31:2-3; John 6:44, 65; 14:6). But He also imparts joy to the one with whom He is pleased. That joy of the Lord then becomes the strength of the one who obeyed, so that obedience may continue in the one. This explains why we experience for ourselves or observe saints who, for absolutely no visible or appreciable reason, seem to be able to continue down the straight and narrow despite the wind and waves of opposition. In the face of apparent defeat, the one possessing the joy of the Lord continues on in obedience, and with every step, draws closer and closer to the Father.

A personal testimony: My wife and I have possessed that joy and we presently possess that joy. There have been numerous times in our life when there seemed to be no way out. All hope was lost and the afflictions just continued to bear down upon us. But each moment, we maintained our trust in the Lord, choosing not to be crushed by our circumstances; and each moment passed and we were not destroyed. (2 Corinthians 4:7-9). We testify that an unwavering trust in the Lord brings a strength that only comes from heaven. When that strength comes He simply says, *"Follow Me"* and somehow you can and you do. You can and you do, not because there has come to you an appreciable change in your situation. You can and do because He has given you something of Himself, and that something is His joy. So the strength that you seek today is the strength that comes from above; that comes when the Lord is pleased with one in whom He finds an obedient heart.

But I will share with you an even more valuable experience. One that I pray directs your path to Him even more. On one occasion, when the Lord sent His joy in response to my wife's and my trust and obedience, I responded to Him by saying that I did not want it. I knew what He was giving me. I had received it on previous occasions, but that particular time, I was weary and unwilling to continue to fight to stay in the way of faith. I knew He could and would strengthen me to go on, but I instead just wanted the battle to stop. I rejected the joy that came from Him that was given to be my strength. I immediately felt the weight of my battle and realized the value of what He was giving to me. Within a matter of moments, I reconsidered my selfishness and accepted His joy and continued on. I did this, but I do not recommend trying it, because the flesh is strong and if it wins, you lose.

So again, the four characteristics of the glory that man gives to God are: *Choice* – man chooses whether to give glory to God by choosing to obey Him; *Attribution* – the glory God receives is attributed only to the man who gives Him glory through obedience; *Origination* – the only glory God receives is the glory that begins in Him, His will and His word; and *Strength*- when God is glorified by man's obedience, He radiates His joy back to man and that joy becomes the strength of man to continue to glorify the Lord.

—————— ❦ ——————

Now, before we leave this lesson, there is one additional characteristic of glory we will cover. However, this characteristic is not concerning the glory given, but the glory retained. In the same way that there is darkness or light, righteousness or unrighteousness, death or life, there is either glory given or glory retained. There is no in-between; it is one or the other. If glory is not given to God, then glory is retained by man. Glory given to God begets eternal life; glory retained by man leads to eternal death.

A most frightening warning about retained glory is given to us in the Revelation to John. There, in chapter 18, the Apostle recorded what he saw and heard as to the fall of Babylon. He wrote the following:

> *"Fallen, fallen is Babylon the great! She has become a dwelling place of demons and a prison of every unclean spirit, and a prison of every unclean and hateful bird. For all the nations have drunk of the wine of the passion of her immorality, and the kings of the earth have committed acts of immorality with her, and the merchants of the earth have become rich by the wealth of her sensuality."*

"Come out of her, my people, so that you will not participate in her sins and receive of her plagues; for her sins have piled up as high as heaven, and God has remembered her iniquities. Pay her back even as she has paid, and give back to her double according to her deeds; in the cup which she has mixed, mix twice as much for her. **To the degree that she glorified herself and lived sensuously, to the same degree give her torment and mourning**" (vv. 2-7) (emphasis added).

It would be a disastrous error for man to assume that Babylon is an earthly city, a nation, or some end-of-the-age evil empire or religion. To believe such is to fall victim to the temptation to accuse or blame another and not rightly judge oneself. At this point you might consider re-reading the chapter *The War of the Lord.*

Rightly understood, "Babylon" is every man that lives to please self and not for the glory of God. (Matthew 22:37-40). Babylon is the personification of all that glorifies, worships, and satisfies self. Its infancy is found in the garden of God before man was even created (Isaiah 14: 13-14; Ezekiel 28:13-17) and its manifestation upon the earth was magnified in the days of Nebuchadnezzar's golden statue. (Daniel 3:1-18).

The human heart (Genesis 8:21; Jeremiah 17:9) that worships itself, satisfies itself, and glorifies itself in its sensuality becomes the dwelling place, not of God (John 14:23-24), but of demons and unclean spirits. It is not some ancient religious order or a godless government that has made the merchants of the earth wealthy, but the human heart set on fulfilling its every passion and satisfying its every desire. Throughout human history, nations and kings have risen and fallen in the drunkenness of its iniquities.

According to the Lord's *Glory Ledger* (that is the name I have given to the event described in Matthew 25:31-46), to the same degree that man glorified himself; he will be given torment and mourning. Why? Because to the degree that man glorified himself, he failed to glorify God. *"It shall be done to you according to your faith"* (Matthew 9:29). Remember, with God, glory is the supreme issue.

So in summary, when God in His abundant *mercy* offers man an opportunity to believe Him in the ordinary course of man's existence, and such a man *chooses* to have *faith* in God and that faith produces *obedience* to God's will, then God supplies His *grace* to then accomplish His intended purpose in that man. When His will is thus accomplished, He is *glorified* by the one through whom it was accomplished and He in turn gives *joy* so that the relationship may continue to grow.

The verse from the top of our reading is taken from the account of the healing of the blind man. As Jesus was passing by this man who was blind from birth, His disciples asked Him whether it was the man's sin or the sin of his parents that caused him to be born in such a condition. Jesus responded that it was neither. He explained that the man was in such a condition *"so that* the works of God might be displayed in him" (John 9:3). When Jesus saw the man in the days following his receiving sight, He said to the man, *"Do you believe in the Son of Man?"* The man asked, "Who is He, Lord, that I may believe in Him?" Jesus said, "He is the one who is talking with you." The man believed and worshipped Him. (vv. 35-38).

In light of our present understanding, "the works of God" displayed in the man was not that he received sight (the by-product of obedience), but that he entered into relationship with the Light of the world (the purpose of obedience). (v. 5). Yesterday you may not have described the condition of being born blind as the mercy of God. Hopefully, today you see this blind condition as the invitation to trust, obey, and glorify the Lord. Remember, "it is God who is at work in you, both to will and to work for His good pleasure" (Philippians 2:13).

At the culmination of the Lord Jesus' earthly work He said to His Father, "I glorified You on the earth." We know He was not lying and we know why He could say that. So, if you are reading this chapter you have an opportunity today and every day to make the same statement to the Lord God before you lie down to sleep. Each day you *will* choose either to be persuaded or led by the circumstances and situations of your human existence, or you *will* choose, in those circumstances and situations, to trust, obey, and please God.

What will be the culmination of your day: glory given; or glory retained?

Chapter 18

The Man in the Middle –
Living as a son of God

Scripture Readings:

"For the Lord gives wisdom; from His mouth come knowledge and understanding" (Proverbs 2:6).

"How blessed is the man who finds wisdom and the man who gains understanding" (Proverbs 3:13).

"There is a way which seems right to a man, but its end is the way of death" (Proverbs 16:25).

"Trust in the Lord with all your heart and do not lean on your own understanding" (Proverbs 3:5).

"Peter took Him aside and began to rebuke Him, saying, 'God forbid it, Lord! This shall never happen to You.' But He turned and said to Peter, 'Get behind Me, Satan! You are a stumbling block to Me; for you are not setting your mind on God's interests, but man's'" (Matthew 16:22-23).

"But I hope in the Lord Jesus to send Timothy to you shortly, so that I also may be encouraged when I learn of your condition. For I have no one else of kindred spirit who will genuinely be concerned for your welfare. For they all seek after their own interests, not those of Christ Jesus" (Philippians 2:19-21).

In light of our chosen Scripture readings, several questions arise for our consideration. The first question is, do we understand understanding and if so, have we acquired it? The second question is, do we know God's interests? Finally, if we know God's interests, have we set our mind on His interests, or do we seek after our own? At first glance these may seem rather disparate topics.

However, they are inescapably related and ultimately enlightening to the thirsty soul. Addressing these questions and arriving at an honest answer to each is the focus of our present endeavor. We will only be the better for having done so. (2 Corinthians 13:5).

It would be most profitable for us to begin our endeavor by ascertaining the interests of God; for if we never come to learn His interests we shall never come to learn Him. If we fail to learn Him we will never gain understanding, and without understanding we will be left to live by the futility of our minds. On the other hand, we cannot begin to know the interests of God without understanding. So there we will begin.

Incline your heart

True personal fulfillment is found in understanding. Without it we wander aimlessly seeking out purpose and meaning. With it we embrace peace and contentment. All men at some level search for understanding. Because understanding is elusive, few find it. Those that do find understanding inherit life.

Every occurrence in the human experience is appraised either naturally or spiritually. Only those occurrences that are appraised spiritually can lead one to possess understanding, as understanding is only spiritual and it only comes by way of revelation from God. (Proverbs 2:6; John 16:13).

A natural appraisal comes by way of the human intellect. It is secured by accumulating information from the physical senses and formulating assumptions and drawing conclusions that do not contradict sound reason.

The man who appraises life's occurrences naturally, trusts in his reasoning and deems any spiritual consideration to be foolishness in the face of fact. (1 Corinthians 2:14). Though his stance regarding the spiritual may never be verbalized (out of a sense of religiosity), the natural man's rejection of any spiritual consideration is seen unequivocally in his actions; he will only *do* what his mind can accept. (Matthew 26:14-16). The man who lives according to a natural appraisal can never please God, for his subsequent actions are without faith and hostile toward God. (Romans 8:5-8; Hebrews 11:6).

An example of this progression is found in the sons of Israel after they spied out the land of Canaan. When they entered the land to spy it out, they saw that *"the people who lived in the land were strong, and that the cities were fortified and very large"* (Numbers 13:28). They also saw the Nephilim in the land. (v.33). Based on what they observed, they *"became like grasshoppers in [their] own sight*, and [in the sight of the Nephilim]. Their fear of the sons of Anak then led them to disregard the command of the Lord to enter in and take the land that He promised to Abraham, Isaac, and Jacob. (Genesis 15:7; Exodus 6:4; Deuteronomy 1:6-8; 3:18; Numbers 13:17–33). As the sons of Israel have here demonstrated, the primary objective of a natural appraisal of things (circumstances or information) is to please and protect the interests of man. (Numbers 14:1-4)

Conversely, a spiritual appraisal is made as a result of the spirit of the man hearing God. The hearing is with the heart (non-physical), not the ear. (Jeremiah 31:33). Even when the ear hears the words of God, the heart must listen and agree. (Ezekiel 12:2; Matthew 11:15; Mark 4:20; John 3:11) Its primary objective is to please and glorify God. (Colossians 1:10; 1 Thessalonians 4:1). Its primary outcome is that man gains understanding.

Unlike a natural appraisal, a spiritual appraisal is not in the least bit dependent upon human intellectual capacity or religious learnedness. (Matthew 18:1-3; Luke 2:46-47). We need only to compare Peter and Nicodemus to see that scholarly or religious attainment does not even begin to prepare the man to understand the most elementary of spiritual matters, and that beginning as a gruff sinful fisherman does not prevent one from gaining the most notable of divine revelations. (John 3:1-12; Mark 8:29-30). Finally, the man who appraises and understands occurrences spiritually, sees and understands all things (2 Timothy 2:7), yet places a value on the natural only to the measure he is directed to by the Spirit. The result being that, if directed by the Spirit to completely disregard the natural appraisal of things, the spiritual man can and will place no value on what the human intellect may provide or demand, recognizing that fact does not equate to truth. (Matthew 14:28-29; John 11:39-44; 1 Corinthians 2:12-13).

Consequently, understanding is a product of assessing the human experience spiritually and not naturally, and acquiring revelation from God as a result of the spiritual assessment. The man so doing must then live pursuant to the revelation received if the understanding is to be of any value to him. Understanding is valuable to the one who gains it when that understanding leads to living in agreement with God's will.

Because a very small percentage of humanity appraises their existence spiritually, it would follow that very few people have acquired understanding. This is so despite the universally accepted position that when man has a firm grasp of the natural appraisal of things (is intellectually advanced in a matter) that he has understanding. It is this prideful error that allows man to think of himself as god (not in the sense of the creator of all things, rather in a particular matter) and therefore place himself on the throne of his heart as sovereign, rejecting the Lordship of God. This is all done at the subconscious level, because very few people are arrogant enough to speak it.

If you consider this to be implausible, just recall the last time you said in the solitude of your thoughts, that what you considered to be the best plan of action in any particular matter is the one you have come up with and not the one God has given, whether He stated it directly to you or through another for you. (Proverbs 3:5; 16:25). Because you thought your plan best and you understood your plan, you then proceeded with your plan. However, you proceeded in error because God has not spoken, or if He has spoken you have not appraised your experience spiritually so as to obtain understanding. The human experience is not about simply living a self-determined life, although most of humanity lives this way. The human existence is about gaining understanding so that life can be lived in such a manner that is pleasing to the Lord. (Colossians 1:9-10). Therefore, be wise and *"incline your heart to understanding"* (Proverbs 2:2).

Walk the Earth,
Look to Heaven

Undoubtedly, the life that Jesus lived in the flesh was a life founded upon understanding, not a natural appraisal of things. For instance, after fasting forty days in the wilderness following His baptism, Jesus was tempted by Satan to turn stones into bread so that He could appease His hunger. Jesus responded to the temptation by declaring that,

> *"Man shall not live on bread alone, but on every word that proceeds out of the mouth of God"* (Matthew 4:4).

Here we witness that Jesus' actions were directed not by an appraisal of natural conditions (extreme hunger and fatigue), but by the will of God. We say the "will of God" and not the word of God, because Satan, in his second temptation, used "the word of God" to tempt Jesus to "step out in faith." Jesus responded to this temptation by declaring the will of God as evidenced by the word of God. (Matthew 4:6-7). True understanding hears and obeys the word of God when the word of God is in line with the will of God. This requires the hearer to know the will of God at all times. This comes only by complete surrender and trust. Caution must be taken not to pick and choose Scripture to fit a condition. To do so is to act on a natural and not a spiritual appraisal; to act on what

He has said and not on what He is saying. The former is self-serving and leads to death; the latter is obedience and gives Life.

Even as a child Jesus was guided by understanding. When He was only twelve He remained in Jerusalem following the Feast of the Passover. When His parents, unaware of this, discovered that He was not in their caravan, they returned to Jerusalem days later and *"found Him in the temple, sitting in the midst of the teachers, both listening to them and asking them questions"* (Luke 2:46). He said to His astonished parents, *"Did you not know that I had to be in My Father's house"* (2:49-50)?

And people who neither knew Him personally nor believed in Him recognized that He was other than natural in His understanding and approach to the things of daily life. Take for example the fisherman who worked all night and caught nothing, but at Jesus' instruction, put his nets out again and caught so many fish that the catch nearly sunk two boats. (Luke 5:1-11). Or consider the religious leader, who came to Jesus saying, *"Rabbi, we know that You have come from God as a teacher; for no one can do these signs that You do unless God is with him"* (John 3:2).

Everything that Jesus did or thought was the result of Him *first* hearing His God and Father. The thoughts that Jesus would have about a situation were whatever the Father's thoughts were about that situation. If the Father stayed, He stayed. If the Father went, He went. His heart was found to be *always* in agreement with the Father's will. (Luke 22:42). By God's own words, Jesus was pleasing to Him, and Jesus lived always to glorify the Father only. (2 Peter 1:17; John 17:4)

His Father was His portion and His inheritance. (Exodus 28:1; Numbers 18:20; Matthew 4:4). He trusted everything to Him and whatever would be needed would be found in His Father, especially the things that concerned Him personally. Consider the words Paul wrote to Timothy,

"No soldier in active service entangles himself in the affairs of everyday life, so that he may please the one who enlisted him as a soldier" (2 Timothy 2:4).

No one personified this truth more than Jesus. He was the ultimate soldier. He fully understood and lived by the reality that as Son, He was a bondservant and soldier unto the Lord. (John 6:38). By being a soldier unto the Lord He would be in service to the Lord God, and He would have no concern for His own affairs (Romans 15:3), for those affairs were now His Father's concern.

This understanding that Jesus possessed and the resultant life He lived were not the result of any scholarly endeavor or attained religious office or rank. Instead, His daily spiritual appraisal and understanding were directly related to His continual surrender to and trust in God. This is the example that He has given to man: walk the earth, but look to heaven. And this should have been most evident to those closest to Him, His disciples. (John 6:68-69; Philippians 2:5-8).

———————

Everything that Jesus did was purposed by God to reveal and work out the Lord God's interest, primarily in Jesus' disciples and secondarily in mankind. His purpose toward the disciples was to make them sons by establishing in their hearts the Fatherhood of God. Jesus did so primarily by revealing Himself. (John 14:7-11). He revealed Himself by revealing His identity. Sonship to the heavenly Father was His identity. (John 5:18-24; 10:22-38). His identity was His purpose (Matthew 26:63-66), and that purpose was to give His Father more of Himself; more sons. (John 17:7-9, 16, 18; Romans 8:14, 29; Galatians 3:26).

From His birth, it was about His identity. (Matthew 1:23; 2:15; 3:17; 4:6; John 1:49-51). Even before He chose a single disciple, He was revealing His identity. (John 1:47-51). Everything He did thereafter was purposed to show the Twelve who He was and, by the will of God, who they were to be through Him. (John 17:6-8, 17-19; Genesis 1:26-31; Ephesians 1:5; Hebrews 4:3b). To accomplish this He used the natural to give birth to the spiritual, continually undertaking to transform these natural men into spiritual men. (Matthew 14:29; John 11:14-15; Galatians 4:19).

It began at Cana of Galilee when He turned water to wine at a wedding. That day He used the natural (the wedding feast ran out of wine) to reveal Himself to His disciples as their Purification. (John 2:11). He did this by juxtaposing their beliefs and traditions with Himself. It was no accident that Jesus instructed the servants to fill waterpots used for the Jewish custom of purification. Those waterpots served a significant religious and social purpose in the Jewish culture, especially as it related to eating and drinking. (Mark 7:1-5; Acts 10:14). When Jesus instructed the servants to fill the purification pots, and then turned that water into wine which would thereafter be consumed as drink by the wedding guests, He brought to the forefront the disciples' trust in the Law and the traditions of their elders.

It would have not been lost to the disciples or the servants that He had turned water into wine in the containers used for washing instead of drinking. This adds significance to John 2:9 which states, that the headwaiter "did not know where the wine came from." Had he known of its origin he certainly would not have tasted it, much less served it. Furthermore, for those present at the wedding, including the disciples, it was understood that the water in the pots was what purified, and that from the outside. Yet, Jesus turned the purification water into wine, to be consumed. This would become very significant later in Jesus' ministry when He, on the night before His trial and crucifixion, handed these same disciples a cup filled with wine and said,

> "*Drink from it, all of you; for this is My blood of the covenant, which is poured out for many for forgiveness of sins*" (Matthew 26:28).

Again, the pots, and the water in the pots, meant something to the disciples. Jesus, by using those pots and turning the water into wine, turned their laws and traditions on their head and revealed to the disciples an aspect of Himself though they yet did not understand. (Hebrews 8:13).

The purposefulness of Jesus' actions in Cana is continued throughout His ministry to the Twelve, as on two rather remarkable days that are not unknown by many. The events of these two days rank high on the list of miracles that Jesus performed in Israel. So impactful were the events that many since have lived in the quiet hope that they too would be able to accomplish as much in their lifetime.

Each of these days began like so many before them; multitudes of people following Jesus wherever He went, waiting to see what He would do and wanting to hear what He would say. On one of those particular days, Jesus was in the countryside near Bethsaida. (Luke 9:10). He had just traveled from Jerusalem where He healed a lame man at the pool of Bethesda. (John 5:1-9). As was His custom, He sat among the people and began teaching them about the kingdom of God and healing those who were ill.

As the evening drew near and the multitude grew larger, His disciples asked Him to send the people into the surrounding villages to find lodging and food. But Jesus responded saying to His disciples, *"You give them something to eat"* (Luke 9:12-13)! The Twelve then suggested to Him that they go and buy food for all the people because they only had with them five loaves and two fish. (Matthew 14:17). One Gospel account records that Jesus asked one of His disciples, *"Where are we to buy bread, so that these may eat?"* That disciple answered saying, *"Two hundred denarii worth of bread is not sufficient for them, for everyone to receive a little*" (John 6:5, 7).

In each of the Gospel accounts of this particular day Jesus then took "*the five loaves and the two fish, and looking up to heaven, He blessed them, and broke them, and kept giving them to the disciples to set before the people. And they all ate and were satisfied*" (Matthew 14:19; Luke 9:16-17; John 6:11). It was said that over five thousand people were there that day. (Matthew 14:21).

On the second of those particular days Jesus was near the Sea of Galilee, within the region of Decapolis. (Mark 7:31). He had just spent the previous three days in the area healing "*those who were lame, crippled, blind, and mute*" (Matthew 15:30, 32). As Jesus looked upon the crowd that followed Him, He conveyed to His disciples the compassion that He had for the people because they had been with Him for three days and had nothing to eat. He said to His disciples, "*I do not want to send them away hungry*" (Matthew 15:32). His disciples answered Him saying, "*Where will anyone be able to find enough bread here in this desolate place to satisfy these people?*" (Mark 8:4).

Jesus then asked His disciples how many loaves they had and they responded that they had seven loaves and a few fish. (Matthew 15:34; Mark 8:5-7). He took the loaves and fish, gave thanks and gave the loaves and fish to His disciples to distribute to the people. (Matthew 15:36). When everyone had eaten and were satisfied there were seven large baskets full of broken pieces. (v.37). It was said that about four thousand people were there that day. (Mark 8:9).

What each of these days possessed of the interest of God and for the eternal benefit of mankind was for the most part lost to the spectacular. The primary cause for this loss was the disciples' negligence in failing to understand and apprehend God's interests in the matter. This is as true for man today as it was for the disciples then. As a point of emphasis and clarification, a reading of the Scriptural account of these two days as being days in which the Lord miraculously fed multitudes of people with only a few fish and loaves is a natural appraisal. This is what man saw, but this is not what God was doing. If this is what God was doing then He would be at best hypocritical and unrighteous in His subsequent rebuke of both the disciples and the multitudes when they concerned themselves with a lack of bread on the boat and desiring more bread the next day, respectively. (Matthew 16:5-12; John 6:26-58).

If we were today to judge whether the disciples possessed understanding on the two subject days, our judgment would have to be that they did not. On that day in the countryside near Bethsaida and on that day in the region of Decapolis, Jesus purposefully led His disciples into a situation where a multitude of people were in need of food. When the opportunities presented themselves, the disciples were invited to act like sons of the Most High God; to imitate that which they had witnessed from Jesus in the days and months before. They were invited to abandon themselves to the Father and be the conduit through which the Father would act. (Psalm 103:7). To do so, the disciples would have to put aside all unbelief. They would have to believe Him without seeing anything; to observe the temporal, but behold and take confidence in the spiritual; to look beyond the need and see the supply. They would have to "KNOW" in the face of all physical evidence to the contrary. (Daniel 3:16-18). But this is not what occurred.

On each occasion, the disciples naturally appraised the situation, gathered the available information and arrived at the logical conclusion – "It cannot be done." ["*Where are we to find enough bread?*"] They stood before the Lord defeated, lacking understanding, and completely unaware of the interests of God. They did not obey the command of the Lord. Instead, they reasoned, they questioned, and they cowered in unbelief. They could do nothing other, for they walked as mere men. (Mark 8:17-18, 21; 1 Corinthians 3:1-4).

Had the disciples surrendered their unbelief and trusted fully in the Lord; had they appraised each of those days spiritually instead of naturally, they would have gained understanding, leading them to know the interests of God in the moment; not that hungry people needed food, but that they become sons, sons of the kingdom. (1 John 3:1). But sadly, they did not understand this.

They did not comprehend that at all times and in all things, Jesus was both revealing His identity and forming theirs. With the feeding of the multitudes and with the changing of the water to wine, Jesus revealed Himself as the Bread of Life and the Wine of the new covenant. With all that Jesus brought to His disciples He was teaching them to know the interest of His Father; the making of sons.

And it is more than just the making of sons. For the making of sons has a further purpose. And that further purpose brings joy of the Father. That further purpose is that He might glorify his sons. Almost every Christian would contend that the primary reason for man's existence is so that man can and would glorify the Lord God. However, that is not the case. Although it is right that every man glorify God, God did not need man to receive glory, for He receives glory from all of creation and has from the foundations of the earth. No, man was not created to give God glory. Man was created so that God could glorify man. Not just any man. The man that God glorifies is the man that has become a son. This is why God has purposed to and is at work in the world to produce sons; so that He may glorify them. (John 17:20-22 ["*I do not ask on behalf of these alone, but for those also who believe in Me through their word; that they may all be one; even as You, Father, are in Me and I in You, that they also may be in Us. The glory which You have given Me I have given to them, that they may be one, just as We are one*"]; Romans 8:16-17 ["*The Spirit Himself testifies with our spirit that we are children of God, and if children, heirs also, heirs of God and fellow heirs with Christ, if indeed we suffer with Him so that we may also be glorified with Him*"]; 2 Thessalonians 2:14 ["*that you may gain the glory of our Lord Jesus Christ*"]; 2 Timothy 2:10 ["*so that they also may obtain the salvation which is in Christ Jesus and with it eternal glory*"]; Hebrews 2:10 ["*in bringing many sons to glory*"]; 1 Peter 5:1, 4 ["*and a partaker also of the glory that is to be revealed.... And when the Chief Shepherd appears, you will receive the unfading crown of glory"*]). The personal examination then becomes, now that I have understanding and I know what the interests of God are, do my interests line up with His such that I will be glorified by God? An honest look into my life will reveal the answer.

Quietness of Soul

Any living done by man that is not in the path of sonship is not in line with the interests of God. This is true both in thought and deed. In speaking of His Sonship to His disciples, Jesus often described to them its characteristics like abandonment, surrender, trust, faith, obedience, love, and glory. He spoke of always being about His Father's business. (Luke 2:49). He explained, as well as demonstrated, that He could do nothing of His own accord, but that He did only as the Father showed Him. (John 5:30; 12:49-50; Matthew 4:3-4; 12:50). In a not so subtle way, Jesus showed that sonship and thus glory is not for every man. It is only for the man who utterly surrenders everything to the Divine Father and lives a life as He lived; obediently. (Philippians 2:8).

When man gains understanding so as to know the interests of God, it is evidenced by his life, the same as it was evidenced in the life of Jesus. This is demonstrated in such a life most noticeably and accurately by the presence of undisturbed spiritual composure and an absence of temporal ownership. This is vastly different than contemporary Christian thought that holds that such things as ministry activity, speaking in tongues, reading your Bible, material blessings, and church attendance are the obvious proofs of knowing God.

When identifying sons from among men, God is not knocking on church doors to see who is inside or looking into your financials to check your credit score. Instead, He is about finding a soul that is not attached to this world and a soul that is so at rest in Him that it is quieted to all but the sound of His voice. (2 Chronicles 16:9). It is this one who qualifies as a son and it is this son who is then positioned to be glorified by the Father.

Quietness of soul finds peace and contentment in God. It dispels all anxieties and fears. It maintains its hold on belief and trust in Him. There is no value given to the temporal condition, good or bad. If such a man finds himself appointed as a king among men, or led into a lion's den, a vat of boiling oil, or a furnace of blazing fire, his soul remains quieted by the knowledge of the Lord and His sovereignty over all things, including his life. There are neither highs nor lows, but all is well with the soul. (Psalm 62:5-6)

Besides being one of the evidences of being a son, quietness of soul has the practical benefit of maintaining the heart in a constant state of hearing and readiness. When the soul is quieted, His voice is magnified and His will is known. The sounds of distraction and temptation are silenced by the stillness of His voice. As a result, the probability of disobedience goes down dramatically, if not completely.

The opposite is true as well. When the soul is disturbed of its rest, it is impossible to hear God. When the focus is on the wind and the waves and not the words of the Lord, the circumstances overwhelm and the only thing that is heard is the flesh screaming for God to move. (Mark 4:38). Quietness of soul makes room for confidence in Him and evicts all fear of the known and unknown.

Jesus manifested this spiritual composure in every circumstance. When He was offered the kingdoms of the world, He was not moved in His soul. (Luke 4:5-7). When His dear friend was near death, He was not moved in His soul. (John 11:3-4). When His own disciple betrayed Him, He was not moved in His soul. (Mark 14:18). When they spat upon Him and beat Him, He was not moved in His soul. (Matthew 26:67). Regardless of what was presented Him, Jesus found no attachment to this world that would disrupt His communion with His Father. In Him, God found quietness of soul. In God, Jesus found everything He needed. This is what must be evidenced in any man who would desire to be called "son" by God.

Finally, there is probably nothing more evidencing of a son that is in line to be glorified by God than an absence of temporal ownership. It is this one who, by his free will places himself, not in the position to receive from God, but in the position to provide from God to another. It is one who forsakes all that he has so that he may glorify the One to whom he has surrendered. (Philippians 2:5-7). In other words, the man of understanding who is living a life pleasing to the Lord is a man who lives in the middle; between God and man; between heaven and earth. He is the man who can, because of his relationship to God (as son), place all that concerns him into the hands of the One whom he serves, and be the instrument to pass to man all that God desires to provide.

To visualize this, imagine a vertical line stretching from heaven to earth at the top of which stands the Lord and at the bottom stands all of mankind. God knows those at the bottom need what He has to offer them. Those at the bottom know nothing. (John 3:16). In the middle voluntarily stand the sons of God. The sons of God understand they have need of nothing because they belong to God. They understand that they are not of this world. (John 17:16; 18:36). They are strangers in a foreign land; aliens and sojourners, "*having nothing yet possessing all things*" (2 Corinthians 6:10) (Leviticus 25:23; 1 Peter 2:11). They consider nothing as their own and are willing to "*suffer the loss of all things, and count them but rubbish so that they may gain Christ*" (Acts 4:32; Philippians 3:8). Their only concern is to do the will of Him who speaks.

When God is looking for those whom He will glorify, He is not looking at the bottom. He is not looking into the sea of humanity. He is looking at the middle, where there are men who have left the world behind and followed after Him. The only way to be in the middle is to move from the bottom. To do so, you must know God, not as Provider, or Deliverer, or any one or several things. You must know God as Everything and the Only thing. Then you will move to the middle and abandon your place as a potential recipient, instead becoming an instrument of Him. The reality of moving to the middle is that as His instrument you partake not of part of what He gives, but of all of what He gives, in the same way that a shofar is touched by every breath, every syllable, every note of the One who blows it, while the hearers of the shofar only hear part, based upon their capacity to hear and their relationship to the One using the shofar.

The challenge before us today is to be a shofar of the Lord; to move to the place where we will be found in line with the interests of God, and qualified to share in the glory of the Lord. To do this we must stop living in continual anxiety, fear, and unbelief. We must re-evaluate our trust in temporal possessions, as so much of human life today, especially in religious circles, considers someone blessed by God if they have much in the way of material possessions.

Jesus is at work in our lives to produce sons for His Father, just as He was at work in the lives of the disciples. We can live a natural life and completely miss out on what God is doing. Or, we can join Him in His work by first inclining our hearts to understanding. Then by gaining understanding of the Father's interest and making His interest our own, surrender ourselves completely to Him, and with quietness of soul live a life here upon the earth, always looking to heaven, with the expectation that doing so will qualify us to receive glory from the Father.

This is the will of God, but it is also the choice of man. What will you choose?

✦

Chapter 19

OUT OF DARKNESS

Scripture Readings:

"For you were formerly darkness, but now you are Light in the Lord; walk as children of Light" (Ephesians 5:8).

"I am the Light of the world; he who follows Me will not walk in the darkness, but will have the Light of life" (John 8:12).

"I have come as Light into the world, so that everyone who believes in Me will not remain in darkness" (John 12:46).

"But you are a chosen race, a royal priesthood, a holy nation, a people for God's own possession, so that you may proclaim the excellencies of Him who has called you out of darkness into His marvelous light" (1 Peter 2:9).

As we shared in the introduction, this book is an account of our experience in coming to know the truth of the Lord. By no means do we contend that we know everything of Him, for we fully anticipate learning more each moment that we walk with Him. But we do contend that what we have learned of Him, we know, and what we now know of Him is far different than what we knew of Him previously. Looking back over the Lord's dealings with us, two things have become very clear. First, in His mercy He took us out of darkness. Not the darkness that is common to all humanity (Romans 3:23), but the darkness that is far worse; the darkness that abides in the hearts of those who pledge an allegiance to a God whom they know not; the darkness of a false, religious knowledge of Him.

This darkness is the condition being addressed by God when He spoke to the prophet Ezekiel. The Lord said to him,

> *"Son of man, I am sending you to the sons of Israel, to a rebellious people who have rebelled against Me; they and their fathers have transgressed against Me to this very day. I am sending you to them who are stubborn and obstinate children, and you shall say to them, 'Thus says the Lord God.' As for them, whether they listen or not—for they are a rebellious house—they will know that a prophet has been among them. And you, son of man, neither fear them nor fear their words, though thistles and thorns are with you and you sit on scorpions; neither fear their words nor be dismayed at their presence, for they are a rebellious house. But you*

shall speak My words to them whether they listen or not, for they are rebellious" (Ezekiel 2:3-7).

This darkness proclaims to know the Lord and serve the Lord, but in reality is in complete rebellion against Him. Not unlike King Saul when he spared King Agag. (1 Samuel 15).

Consider the darkness of Israel in the days of Christ. It was not a darkness of the Gentiles that polluted the souls of God's people. It was the darkness of their knowledge of Him. This is illustrated throughout the gospels as the Lord confronted the beliefs of the Pharisees; as in the case when Jesus and His disciples ate from the grain fields. It was on the Sabbath that they picked and ate of the grain. When the Pharisees saw this they condemned the Lord for doing what was not lawful. In response, Jesus reminded them of when David and his men *"entered the house of God, and ate the consecrated bread"* (Matthew 12:4). He then rebuked them saying,

> *"[I]f you had known what this means, 'I DESIRE COMPASSION, AND NOT A SACRIFICE,' you would not have condemned the innocent"* (Matthew 12:7).

Again, on the Sabbath, Jesus gave sight to a man born blind. The Pharisees sought to condemn Jesus to death for blasphemy for doing what was not lawful to do on the Sabbath. (John 9). On a third occasion, He rebuked their self-righteousness in condemning the adulterous woman, but sent the woman away in freedom, with the hope of eternal life, if she would but continue without sin. (John 8:1-11).

In His mercy the Lord transferred us from the darkness of our knowledge of Him. He did so by allowing the Truth to be shone. As we opened our hearts to His mercy, He opened our eyes to see the Truth. As we saw the Truth, we repented and repented and repented. Not for the same thing again and again, but for each thing He revealed that was in error. Each time He revealed a wrongly held belief, He brought us out of the religious deception and into His Light. Once we knew the Truth we could begin to live the Truth.

And this is the second thing that has become so clear. The manifestation of the sons of God is not some apocalyptic event or end-time mystery that the Church should be waiting for. The manifestation of the sons of God is nothing other than the earthly completion of the work of God in the lives of men. It is the revelation of the Church; of the body of Christ. It is revealed when a man becomes the Light, becomes the Truth. Not because of himself, but because of the Life and the Truth that dwells within him. He is the Light that shines out of darkness.

Today, we live as sons of God, as Light shining out of darkness, as He Himself lives in us. For it is no longer we that live, but He that lives His life in us. (Galatians 2:20). Every man chooses between the Light and the darkness. (John 3:19-21). There is no neutral ground. It is our sincere hope and prayer that as you close this book, you open your heart to the Lord to have Him work in you His good pleasure. It is the hardest thing you will ever do. It is the most rewarding thing you will ever do.

The time is now, for the manifestation of the sons of God.

End Notes

Chapter 4

1. Sun Tzu. Art of War. New York: Delacorte, 1983. Print.

Chapter 6

1. "disillusionment". Oxford Dictionaries. Oxford University Press, n.d. Web. 18 June 2013. <http://oxforddictionaries.com/us/definition/american_english/disillusionment>.

Chapter 8

1. "satisfy." *Merriam-Webster.com*. Merriam-Webster, 2015. Web. 11 March 2015.

Chapter 9

1. "confused." *Merriam-Webster.com*. Merriam-Webster, 2015. Web. 18 May 2015. - This chapter is limited to discussing confusion that is not brought on by bodily injury, substance abuse or other medical reasons.

Chapter 12

1. "canonical." *Dictionary.com*., 2015. Web. 17 May 2015.

Printed in the U. S. A.

www.ingramcontent.com/pod-product-compliance
Lightning Source LLC
Chambersburg PA
CBHW060010050426
42448CB00012B/2684